Organisation Development Systems

About the Authors

Vinayshil Gautam: Everything which Prof. Gautam says or writes carries the indelible mark of his original thinking. It is difficult to ignore his views and conviction. As the First Head of the Department of Management Studies, IIT(D); Founder Director of IIM(K); Leader, Consulting Team, IIM (Shillong); Past President, ARTDO International (Manila); Ex-Director, IFTDO (Geneva); Past Chairman, All India Board of Management Education, AICTE, he has carried his pioneering zeal with high professionalism. Having been invited for talks from Montreal to Melbourne and Caracas to Tokyo he has utilised the occasion to test his ideas for nearly two dozen management books and over a hundred papers, several of which have won awards. He has lectured at Universities such as Sussex, Cambridge, London, Brunell in UK; Dominican, Duke, Minnesota, Penn State in USA; York, Toronto in Canada. He is currently the A Al_Sager Chair Emeritus Professor at IIT(D) as faculty and carries various fellowships including that of Royal Asiatic Society (London).

Dr. Surinder Batra is Professor and Area Chairperson for Information Technology & Systems at ITM, Ghaziabad. He is an MBA from Faculty of Management Studies, University of Delhi and Ph.D. from IIT, Delhi, and a recipient of Dr. V. K. R. V. Rao Gold Medal and Prof. A. Das Gupta Gold Medal from Delhi University. Earlier, he has been the Principal Consultant of Centre for Interactive Management India (CIMI). He has also been Group Leader and Senior Consultant with Tata Consultancy Services, Faculty, Administrative Staff College of India, Hyderabad, India. He has authored several papers in IT & Organizational Effectiveness, Knowledge Management and Knowledge-based Development. He has authored four books, two of which were for Asian and Pacific Skill Development Program of ILO. He has been on the panel of experts for Most Admired Knowledge Cities Award constituted by the World Capital Institute. He is also a member of the Scientific Committee of "Information System Dynamics", a long-term project initiated by CIGREF Foundation of France in collaboration with University of Paris-Sud, France.

Organisation Development Systems

(A Study in Organisation Behaviour and Organisation Management)

5th Revised Edition

VINAYSHIL GAUTAM
and
SURINDER K. BATRA

CONCEPT PUBLISHING COMPANY PVT LTD.,
NEW DELHI-110059

ISBN-13: 978-81-8069-829-3 (H.B.)

First Published 1993
Second Edition 2000
Third Edition 2001
Fourth Edition 2007
Fifth Edition 2011

Published and Printed by

Concept
Since 1974

Concept Publishing Company Pvt. Ltd.
Regd. Office:
A/15-16, Commercial Block, Mohan Garden,
New Delhi-110059 (INDIA)
Phones : 25351460, 25351794, *Fax* : 091-11-25357109
Email : publishing@conceptpub.com
Website: www.conceptpub.com

Editorial Office:
H-13, Bali Nagar, New Delhi-110 015, India.

Cataloging in Publication Data--*Courtesy:* D.K. Agencies (P) Ltd. <docinfo@dkagencies.com>

Gautam, Vinayshil.
Organisation development systems : a study in organisation behaviour and organisation management / Vinayshil Gautam and Surinder K. Batra. -- 5th rev. ed.
p. cm.
Includes bibliographical references (p.) and index.
ISBN 9788180698293

1. Organizational change. 2. Organizational behavior. 3. Industrial management. I. Batra, Surinder, joint author. II. Title.

DDC 658.406 23

for

Shri R.K. Upadhyay

CMD, BSNL & TCIL

Preface to the Fifth Revised Edition

The changes in the last five years have been profound in all aspects of organised life. It is natural therefore that the theory and practice of organisations be updated to meet the contemporary and emerging demands. Hopefully, the fifth updated edition of this book will meet the needs of the discerning reader.

The changes are too many to enumerate. They speak for themselves.

A sincere thank you for the readership that keeps this book alive.

July 6, 2011 **Vinayshil Gautam**
New Delhi

Preface to the Fourth Edition

It is five years since the third edition of this book was brought out. It has been out of print for last two years.

My pre-occupation with another title "Digital Imperatives" and various professional and personal priorities made it impossible for me to attend to this task with any degree of attention.

The continued demand for it, however, reached a point, this summer, that became impossible to ignore, any further. Hence this fourth edition.

A new chapter, basically outlining the trend in the last five years has been added in this book as chapter 12. The authors believe it is an important addition to strengthening its leadership position in the designing of course contents for Post Graduate Management education.

It is indeed gratifying to see how the readership has reacted to the book.

August 23, 2006
New Delhi

Vinayshil Gautam

Preface to the Third Edition

The second edition got exhausted much sooner than anticipated. The enthusiasm with which this book has been received is gratifying.

In response to the feedback received, a new chapter dealing with Information Technology and Organizations has been further added to the text. We are convinced that this will enhance the utility of this book. We shall be grateful if the dialogue with the readers would continue, as has been the case in the past.

September 24, 2000 **Vinayshil Gautam**
New Delhi

Preface to the Second Edition

This book was first published in 1993. The first edition got exhausted much quicker than expected. Persistent nature of the demand made it necessary to fall back upon reprints. There were not enough time to revise the text. An interesting aspect of the demand was the requests that came from Singapore or Malaysia. However, six years of change in the organisational management field made it obvious that somewhere a pause was necessary and an enlarged and revised edition be brought out. What you now peruse is the outcome.

Some of the observations made in the text earlier were born out to be realistic. The pressure on the Indian companies has increased in the intervening period and generally then has been the experience of a recession. The BIFR has had various exigencies to deal with and hopefully the world of work should have better days ahead.

One word that confronts the world of work more boldly than ever before is 'competitiveness'. Competitiveness has become necessary for the very act of survival. Survival cannot be insured by blocking others, it can be targetted by putting one's own house in order and strengthening one's own working.

This book is hopefully a small contribution in helping those who seek to understand how organisations work and how to help them to work better.

In the emerging hastened pace of technological change and the widespread technological convergence (that looms large on the horizon of telecommunications) organisations are not only going to metamorphose but are likely to take forms and patterns that were never foreseen. One has to be prepared for it. It is obvious that the first five years of the 21st century will be seminal for the cutting edge of human evolution.

Towards this end it is important to recognise that unlike other disciplines management is a craft. Quintessentially it is a practitioner's art and a science. It revolves around an identifiable framework. That framework is often referred to as the "organisation".

As would be easily recognised, an insight into organisation requires not only an understanding of the motivational processes, of planning, control and co-ordination systems but also of ways of identifying tasks, putting them together to create a job design. Job designs would require certain competencies for task accomplishments. Professionals with those competencies would have to be assigned those jobs. As the nature of the tasks change so must the character of the jobs and necessitating thereby a fresh configurations of human competencies and skills to handle them.

Organisation design therefore becomes a response to a careful diagnosis of the demands made by an organisation's operating context. Here is mission, vision, environment, human characteristics, technology, size, milieu, mental health of and attitude of those that matter—all become relevant to an organisation's success or failure. Ultimately, organisations grow only when they become institutions. The difference is that whereas organisations can be created around activities, institutions demand creation of a value, pursuit of an idea and a reach for the mission.

To operate all this, process issues become significant. That is where, also, the organisation has to be viewed as a system that needs to be continuously developed. The support systems of information flows and identification of decision centres become crucial concerns. The book attempts to deal with some of these issues.

The book has also been enriched by the readership response. This relationship will, one is sure, make for the continued relevance of the effort.

By going through the pages that follow, you become a member of this growing fraternity. To this fellowship, you are cordially invited.

January 3, 1999 **Vinayshil Gautam**
New Delhi

Preface to the First Edition

Writing a preface for this book turned out to be more difficult than I had anticipated. First I wrote out a slightly extended piece which, amongst other things, touched upon some of the paradigms that impact the organisational operations in developing countries in general and India in particular. This was supported by my consulting and research experiences, especially of the large organisations in India. My co-author, Surinder, on reading it shot it down, labelling it as being more of a "post-face" rather than a "pre-face". The comments of a co-author cannot be easily brushed aside!

So, I decided to make the preface briefer and raise certain generic concerns on the function of organisations, annotating it, this time, with my experiences of management development activity, consulting and research in India, Germany, Saudi Arabia and United Arab Emirates. It had the obvious advantages of a comparative perspective. For instance, it is interesting to compare how talk of ISO 9000 has acquired the status of almost an industry in India while in Europe itself, it gets no undue attention. Concerns of quality are poised there on the fringes of innovation and extending the frontiers of machine and service competencies. Quality clearly means different things to different people. In the Middle East, the quantum of revenue from manufacturing being comparatively much lower than that from oil drilling and refining activities (or for that matter even from, services such as of ports) "quality" issues are really focused on time and service efficiencies. It is not surprising, therefore, that the management world seems to be throwing up its own sub-universes. Productivity is another concept doing the rounds. Urgings for higher productivity in an environment remarkably deficient in infrastructure and services is not uncommon. Can the corporate world create, in this part of the world, its own infrastructure? The question may not be such a moot one, with the World Bank urging setting up of captive power plants as an enabling clause for attention! If this is the law of the land, which way are our organisations headed? I recall, in Leipzig, the topic of one of my management development interventions was "Individual's identity in the new *organisational space*". What is the organisational space of our enterprises? These are large questions and by definition, therefore, do not become something to be carpeted under.

It seems to me that in developing countries in general, and India in particular, perceptions and analysis of concerns of organisation management need to be considerably strengthened. Without this basic groundwork no organisation development work can take place and certainly the needs of organisational renewal cannot be suitably responded to. This book is intended to be a humble contribution in that direction so that the average understanding of organisation structure, process and growth get to be further strengthened.

Poised as we are in time at the point of easing out of 1993 and the impending oncoming of 1994, our organisations are at multiple crossroads. All types of choices have to be exercised and quickly at that. It is obvious that of the thousands of corporate enterprises which exist in India today, a substantial number amongst them may not be around after another five years. Reasons of professional delicacy prevent one from naming any of them or hypothesising. Those who know are even talking several of the well known banking organisations as being in the red. How many of them will survive? After "loan-melas" and "loan waiving off" expeditions, is it surprising that the chicken are coming home to roost? Looking for models and answers from the prestigious intellectual centres of other environments may be like looking for "space cooling systems" from factories that specialise in the fabrication of "space heating systems"! We have to look for answers that will be consistent with the historicity of our circumstances, realities of our environment and mindsets that are so uniquely Indian and of "the east".

It is obvious that the urgent issue on the agenda of organisation management and development is that of redefining work itself. With the new tools of managerial work which draw so liberally on techniques of mechanisation, automation and computerisation, it is required that, by definition, structure of "work" itself accounts for these technological variables. This is not to overlook the impact of networking, telecommunication linking facilities and satellites. If the need of organisations of the day is a multi-design job description, are we ready with the profile of the multi-skill worker?

Indeed, restructuring of organisations, *per se*, is itself of limited value unless there are matching changes in administrative procedures and practices at the micro level. Organisations which have attempted the first, without accounting for the second, have succeeded in dramatically raising the level of discontent. Indeed, even restructuring at a larger level, like the one when there is talk of restructuring the public sector enterprises, will remain an exercise of rhetoric unless concomitant changes in company, labour, tax and banking laws are brought about. This is going to be an arduous task. The building blocks of organisations have to be understood. A new architecture of organisational operations have to be conceived and put on the ground. For this, a futuristic perception of intra-organisational and inter-organisational configurations would be much required.

The task is complicated by professionals who, with their rigid mindsets have difficulties in understanding interfaces. Typically, an operations research man tends to take lightly the contribution and sophistication of behavioural sciences and *vice versa*. This weakens both. It prevents a holistic understanding of the complexities of organisational operations. Add this to the situation where, in operational terms, there is what would be called—the dominance of the core discipline. Typically, in a manufacturing unit, the Mechanical Engineers would have preponderant say in the decision-making process to the neglect of even other Engineers, say, typically, the Electrical or the Civil. The result being that the robustness of the decision-making suffers and skewed analysis carries the day. It is obvious that the management of interfaces is going to be the crucial issue of survival of many organisations. The enabling disciplines have to be as professional, manned by as competent personnel as the core discipline. This requires inculcating the approach of strategic thinking and a very careful selection of people in key positions for co-ordinating decisions. In the absence of such norms the stiffling environment, which many today are bothered about in our organisations, will not be solved in operational terms but will continue to sap the utility of organisational dynamics.

Ultimately, creation of values and definition of standards becomes critical. In the absence of this, no real professionalism can be expected in organisational functioning.

Standards, however, cannot be defined until the basic principles are understood and put in operation. Here again this book, it is hoped, will make some contribution in clarifying some of the essentials of organisation management and development.

There is a growing talk of vision, mission and goal orientation in our environment. This is all to the good, but is not enough. Vision needs resources to materialise and above all, a delivery mechanism to be put on the ground. Our organisations will have to increasingly train themselves in fashioning delivery mechanism and move beyond techniques of forecasting, policy formulation and planning. Organisational shelves are full of good plans. What is now needed is a deliberate skill formation for 'making of a practitioner', a manager. The way our organisations answer this question may well be the acid test for their growth and indeed survival. Burdens on this are many.

A public sector undertaking that I had an occasion to be associated with, had approximately 600 peons in a workforce of 3000 and another 400 managers who were just undergraduates. This is a high profile organisation and obviously not an exception in the run-of-the-mill public sector undertakings. There can be multiple ways of looking at this "tooth to tail" ratio and issues of manpower planning. But the central question remains—"did the organisation carry out any job design efforts and document them before recruitments were made?" More centrally, was this even considered to be an issue? Can one live with such situations? Is it not true that an extraordinarily large number of government organisations today, in various parts of the country, are having difficulties in paying regular salaries and some of them are in arrears for over two years? It is our belief that understanding concerns of organisation management and development will help create a more upgraded professional bottom line for action.

Talking of the number of people and manpower ratios, it is natural to reflect upon the issue of grades and promotions. Here too, the underpinning of sound understanding of organisation management and development principles becomes critical. Illustratively, in a given organisation that I had occasion to work for, there were nine grades. Assuming that the top grade was number nine and then each grade be numbered in a declining order, the situation was as follows. Level nine was appointed by the government, so was level eight which consisted of members of the Executive Board. Levels seven to five had really the same types of skill requirements because the tasks were similar. Levels four to one also had similar types of tasks and skills requirements. Thus, it is that if one got into level one he would almost automatically graduate to level four—other things being equal and normal. The only significant assessment was, therefore, from level four to five. After this again there should be smooth sailing to level seven. Decisions on level eight and nine were not internal to the organisation, anyhow. Once this was understood, working out of a promotion policy became a relatively less complicated task.

Effectively, in a very large number of organisations in developing countries in general, and in India in particular, the presence of the government and government-led institutions (typically, institutions dealing with institutional finance) has been extraordinarily large. This has reduced the autonomy of corporate functioning and constrained choices. The typical argument made for such presence has been, truly an enormously large degree of public funding or "preference" available to the given corporate sector enterprise in one form or another. Now that the public exchequer stands "successfully" drained through almost "avaricious" and "callous" over-spending, the issues are more sharply focused. With limited capacity to grant aid, subsidise and give loans from the public exchequer side, there is no real justification of the presence of the government and bureaucracy in running of corporate affairs. Whereas corporations will need to operate in a manner consistent with the "general will" as reflected by the governmental policies, and as the "government" concerns itself more centrally with the act of "governance" rather than business, the corporate sector will have to raise its own resources. For this, a more robust perception of organisational principles is a must.

Obviously, for this a great deal of de-learning, learning and re-learning will be required. In 1985, I had the privilege of serving as the Chairman of a Convention at Vigyan Bhavan set up by Indian Society for Training and Development and the Training Divisions of the Ministry of Personnel, Public Grievances and Pensions on "Learning Strategies". One of the major recommendations of the convention was "If Management of change and transition is going to be a critical issue to future of our organisational functioning, our organisations would have to be put in a learning mould". For this, going back to the fundamentals of organisations is a must. The temptation of flaunting one's own values and assumptions as "standards" simply by virtue of a seemingly powerful appointment one holds, has to be resisted. In all things, an objectivity has to be brought in and scientific standards laid. If this book contributes towards the creation of this value, then the effort would be worthwhile.

3 October, 1993 **Vinayshil Gautam**

Contents

Chapter 1

Nature and Function of Organisations

The Nature of Organisations

This book won't have been written if there were no organisations behind it. Not only the publishers organisation was necessary to take care of publishing the book and marketing it, the autnors themselves had to form an 'Organisation' to design the outline of the book, write individual chapters by dividing responsibilities amongst each other, get a review done and finally handover the completed manuscript to the publishers. The publishers organisation is a formal organisation, while that between the authors is an informal one. Both are critical for bringing out this book.

We are so much in the think of formal and informal organisations in present day life that we often ignore their pervasiveness and don't realise their impact on our lives. Family is the first organisation of which we are members. Our place of work is another organisation or a part of another organisation, where we spend considerable part of our daily working hours. Our customers, vendors, suppliers, agents are parts of various organisations. Our venues of recreation like the club, the sports teams or even the idiot box, TV etc. represent yet another group of organisations. So, organisations are here, there and everywhere influencing our daily life, in fact carving out our own individual daily lifestyles.

Can we do without organisations? The answer is a simple 'no'. Why do we need organisations at all? Perhaps, if each one of us were in a position to satisfy all our individual needs with absolutely no support from others, it would have been possible to live without organisations. However, that is not possible. Our needs are so many (and insatiable at that) that we can't satisfy all through our individual efforts in creating goods and services for meeting them. More importantly, none of us individually have the capabilities to create all goods and services (in whatever quantities we need them) required by us, either from the point of view of skills or resources. Therefore, we need support from others. We join together to form organisations, which are aimed at achieving specific objectives. And thus, organisations are formed.

The formation of organisations is perhaps the most natural trait of human beings. This is one innovative characteristic of human beings which sets them apart from most other living beings (of course, many other life forms carry out organised activities; e.g. witness the march of ants). The act of 'organising' has become ingrained into the psyche of each one of us, so much so that we can't survive without organisations. They become important sociological instruments to meet our sociological needs. Thus, not only do the organisations have economic rationale, they also have a sociological rationale.

Organisations have a political rationale too. We, as human beings, constantly look for ways and means to influence others; we want to play God to others; we seek power the authority. Organisations provide us effective means to wrest power and to exert influence upon others. This influence is supposedly towards the goals of the organisations, which are set by all the members of the organisation. And yet, it is likely that over a period of time the objectives of those yielding power, start dominating the goals of the organisations.

The act of organisations obviously results in defining the roles of individual members. They have to structure themselves in specific manners to best achieve organisational objectives. It becomes necessary to define job responsibilities of individuals, hierarchical relationships amongst the members, accountabilities at individual levels and procedures/work methods required to be adopted. It also becomes necessary to put in position the mechanisms for information flow and communication amongst members (as well as with outsiders) and co-ordinate and control of various tasks being performed in the organisation. Many factors influence the exact nature of the above variables. These include, for instance, the demands of the operating technology, which may dictate the number of organisational members required and the most productive work division amongst them.

One significant consequence of the above organisational phenomena is their constraining effect on the organisational members.

No longer they have a free will (if at all they had a free will prior to becoming organisational members), they have to behave in a particular way, and have to perform in a particular way. These constraints create their own strain on the organisational members, who need to react in some way to keep off the strain, at last temporarily. And we witness new phenomena, such as, industrial relations problems, absenteeism and employee turnover, organisational conflicts, motivational problems and the like. No doubt, while we as organisational members desire a number of benefits from the organisations, we also pay a heavy price for being and remaining organisational members braving all the rough weather, generated by those very phenomena, which are essential for achieving organisational objectives. In the process, we create new needs for us, which may take the steam off, and for satisfying these new needs, we create yet new organisations. For instance, employee unions may get formed to enable organisational members with common interests to get united. Thus, the spiral of organisations and organisational life goes on. We get more and more embroiled into the spider web of organisations.

Characteristics of Organisations

At this stage, it may be a good idea to identify the typical characteristics of all organisations. Firstly, organisations have specific purposes for which they have been created. These purposes may be documented (e.g. Memoranda of Association of Companies) or verbal. It is not necessary, that these purposes should be permanently defined for an organisation; in fact, these can and do change over time. (The ability of organisations to redefine their purpose is a token of their adaptability to environmental needs). However, at any given time, an organisation has to function with a clear purpose, without which it will reduce to a degenerate collectivity.

Organisations have to have organisational members with specific skills through which they contribute in achieving organisational purposes. The possession of these skills is the reason deterre of their being organisational members. The skills need not merely be at an operating level; it is also the supervisory skills, the managerial skills, the customer relations skills and the Government liasioning skills etc. which are critical.

Since, the diversity of skills available in the organisations needs to be made use of most effectively, it is necessary for organisations to have work divisions based on specialisations. This creates the need for group formations, with various groups responsible for certain sub-objectives of the organisation. Each group in itself needs to be bound by formalised work division amongst members, co-ordination of their activities, well defined rules and procedures governing their working relationships and communication modes.

Organisations also need to have hierarchies of authority and accountability. Someone in a group is accountable for the outputs of all members of the group. He or she is vested with a certain degree of authority to be able to plan for, assign tasks, monitor and control group's activities. The members of the group start 'reporting' to him and he in turn reports to another person higher up in the hierarchy.... and so on. The pyramid of the organisation thus takes shape. Today of course, we talk of flat organisations and it is a fact that technology has progressively enabled emergence of flatter hierarchies; however, no technology has as yet eliminated the need for hierarchies in organisations.

The organisations have value systems of their own, which get formed over a period of time, through a mix of the societal value system's influences, imperatives of the organisational technology, size and other variables and the individual styles, beliefs and attitudes of all members, particularly the top management, whose perceptions have the most influence.

These are the typical characteristics of all organisations. Any manager, academician or researcher should take cognizance of these characteristics when dealing with organisations.

At this stage it may be worthwhile to distinguish between structural aspects of organisations and their processes. Drawing an analogy with the human body, the structure represents the anatomy while the processes represent the physiology of an organisation. The structural aspect includes, for instance, job design, work levels, authority relationships and work methods. The processes include, on the other hand, the nature of information flow and communications in the organisation, control and co-ordination functions etc.

It is also important to mention behavioural aspects of organisations, which are akin to the human psychology, continuing the analogy of the organisation with the human body. These include factors such as motivation, leadership, job satisfaction etc.

Figure 1.1 illustrates the three dimensions of organisations mentioned above.

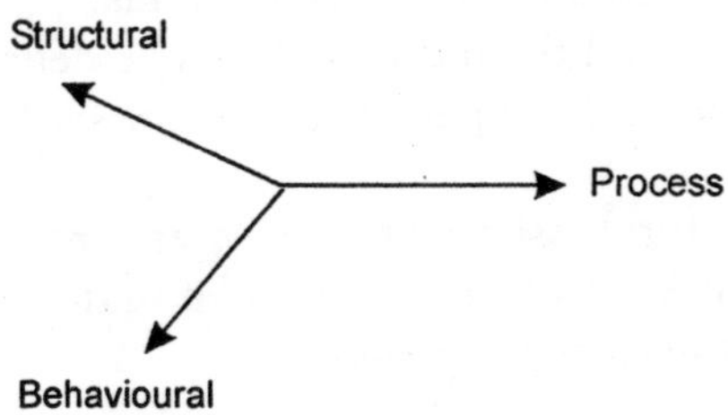

Figure 1.1: Three Dimensions of Organisations

Organisation Structure Related Issues

This book deals with a variety of structure related issues of organisations. The most significant issue, of course, is how to design the most appropriate organisation structure for a given set of organisational objectives. This is currently more of an art than science and is very much in the realm of practising managers and consultants, who rely upon their past experiences and empirical guidelines rather than through sound conceptual frameworks. This issue of designing the appropriate structure subsumes in itself various other issues such as the most desirable interface of the organisation with its external environment, finding a match between the social and technical subsystems and establishing internally compatible authority relationships, work methods and job designs. To be more specific, some of the structure related issues which confront with those who are designing the organisations, managing the organisations, operating in the organisations or dealing with organisations, are as follows:

(a) What is the 'right' hierarchy for the organisation?
(b) What should be the spans of control at various hierarchical levels in the organisation?
(c) How should the line and staff functions be designed and operationalised in the organisation?
(d) What should be the nature of management information system in the organisation?
(e) How should the authority and accountability be distributed in the organisation?
(f) What should be the work methods?
(g) How should the individual jobs be defined?
(h) How should the performance appraisal be conducted?

These structural issues, obviously, are interdependent and present a complex set of problems to be understood and solved by all, who matter in the organisation.

Process Related Issues

The complexity posed by structural issues is further aggravated by the need to establish a right mix of organisational processes, posing issues such as the following:

(a) How should decision making function be carried out in the organisation? To what extent is it possible to grant autonomy to subunits and to what degree, centralised control is necessary?
(b) What should be the communication patterns in the organisation—from top to bottom, from bottom to top,

across horizontal levels, within a group or with other groups?

(c) How should the co-ordination take place amongst constituent units of the organisation?

(d) How should the control be exercised? What control mechanisms should be instituted in the organisation?

Again, this is not a comprehensive list of process related issues of organisations.

Organisation Behaviour

The behavioural dimensions of organisations throw open a variety of issues, which have their origin in the human nature and which can't be ignored by anyone dealing with organisations. Some of the typical issues related to organisational behaviour are as follows:

(a) What is the nature of affiliation of human being with the organisation?

(b) How do the organisational members get motivated or demotivated?

(c) How does the behaviour of organisational members get influenced through interpersonal affiliations, group formations and existence of larger aggregations?

(d) What are the nuances of leadership in organisations?

(e) What games do organisations play?

Perhaps, it is the behavioural aspects of an organisation which are the most uncertain and unpredictable as compared to the structural and process related aspects. These behavioural issues add a new challenge for the managers of the organisations and also make the study of organisations much more interesting.

Organisation Development

Let us face it. Whether we like or not, organisations exist. Some kind of a structure, well defined or not, is there to dictate how things will move in the organisations. Some kind of organisational processes do get instituted in the organisations, depending upon the balance of influence of all members over each other. There exist motivation/demotivation at a certain level, leadership of some sort emerges and some kind of an organisational behaviour, right or wrong, does manifest itself in all surviving organisations. Thus, the organisations do operate at some 'state' at all times. However, it may be changing its state to a more favourable or a less favourable one, with time, depending upon the current mix of all the above types of factors.

However, if organisational effectiveness has to be achieved at all times, it is necessary to institute coping strategies or interventions, which enable the organisations to consciously move from 'chaotic' conditions to those which promote healthy operations, both in the short-term and the long-term. These coping strategies form the subject matter of Organisation Development.

The coping strategies at organisational level are those which are aimed at strengthening the structural aspects and streamlining the processes of organisations. These include, for instance, design interventions, technology assessment, management by objectives, diversification and growth strategies and training and development. At an individual level, coping strategies aim at preparing the individual organisational member to fit into the organisation's structural and process framework, more smoothly. These include techniques such as transactions analysis, counselling, team building, sensitivity training, psychotherapy, psycho-analysis and psychiatric interventions.

There is also a need to stabilise the self-renewal competencies of organisations. This requires developing the capability in the organisation for understanding group problems, managing change and providing for flexibility, creativity and innovation. These are also significant contributions expected from the OD practitioners.

Some Concluding Remarks

This book is entitled 'Organisation Development Systems'. Obviously, a systems approach has been adopted in bringing out organisational issues and their interrelationships. Systems approach, in this context, has been taken to mean, looking at the organisations from a holistic point of view. We are endeavouring to create a systems model of the organisation as an essential framework for analysis. However, it should be recognised that a systems model is a mere model. It is like an artist's sketch of a railway station, which may miss the muzzling buzzlings of the station.

The systems model of the organisation may similarly fail to catch something vital, but unmodellable. Besides, organisations require a dynamic modelling, since they are always in a state of flux.

This is where there will always be a perpetual residual challenge for the OD practitioners.

The second important comment is that organisational issues are location and culture specific. They are dictated by the demands of external environment, which need to be recognised, identified and appropriately dealt with. No cook book solutions to organisational issues exist so far. There are no patented solutions to organisational malaise. All we can do is, outline broad based methodologies which can serve as some guidelines.

Thirdly, the quest of this book at the approach level is to make the reader think and enlarge his conceptual base. This will help the readers in taking conscious position and informed decisions on major issues relating to the organisations they deal with. This is what management is all about.

Fourthly, the nature of organisational theories is largely empirical. All learning in organisation development is experience distilled into concept. Further, not everything can be rationally established.

Lastly, the subject matter of OD requires lateral integration. There is no hierarchy of knowledge, no vertical logic, but a lateral logic. There is a lot of mutual enmeshing of concepts.

Not all the issues affecting organisational effectiveness will ever be known completely. There will always be grey areas. And yet, decisions have to be taken, since organisational problems cannot wait for solutions to develop in theory. This book attempts modestly to provide some answers.

Chapter 2

Individual Organisation Environment Interface

Wheel within a wheel, within a wheel. That is how one can describe the individual organisation environment interface. Individuals as members of the organisation influence and are influenced by organisation structures and processes. Organisations as components of the global environment influence and are influenced by a host of environmental factors such as the technology, the culture and the value system of the environment. This chapter examines the nature of the interface which an individual has with the organisation and which an organisation has with its environment.

Individual and Organisation

From the point of view of an individual, organisational membership is a source of great strength, since organisations help in satisfying a variety of individual's needs, whether economic, social, political or cultural. On the other hand, organisational membership is also a source of considerable strain on the individual, since he is required to confirm to the demands imposed upon him by organisation's structure and processes. This creates a dichotomy for the organisation person; 'to be or not to be' is the continual debate in the mind of the individual. At least one typical response to this eternal debate is the decision of the individual to leave the organisation and join another, apparently for greener pastures. The underlying computation of course appears to be the balance between increased gains and more sacrifices required to be made.

Individual has other responses too, to this debate. In fact, these responses can be as varied as the complexity of the human behaviour itself, which, perhaps, is least understood even today, despite advances in psychology and organisation behaviour. Human behaviour is in fact a complex interplay of the value systems, objectives, processes and motivations of the human being and this manifests itself in multiple, sometimes unpredictable ways.

Some of the characteristics of individuals which, however, are usually observed, in relation to their interface with the organisations are as follows:

Firstly, individuals are simultaneously members of different organisations. For instance, an individual may be a member of a family, employee of a business organisation and activist of a religious sect, simultaneously. He also has the flexibility and discretion to contribute differently to different organisations, to which he belongs simultaneously. Secondly, there exists a 'gaming' phenomenon amongst individuals. This implies that behaviour of one individual is dependent upon the actions and intents of others, and *vice versa*. Thirdly, the very fact of observation of human behaviour, results in a possible change in the behaviour. Thus, there is no guarantee that the observed behaviour will be sustained; chances are that it has already changed, from the time it came under observation. Fourthly, very often, human behaviour tends to follow the dictum of self-fulfilling prophecies. This implies that if a prediction is made about the behaviour of an individual at a particular time, his behaviour is likely to be influenced by that prediction, either towards achieving that prediction or towards negating it.

Where does this lead the organisations to? It appears they are caught in a continual struggle to reconcile with the vagaries of human behaviour. The organisations need to survive and grow; they need to maintain their identity, irrespective of who are and who are not members of the organisation. This they do by 'institutionalising' (prescribing rules and regulations, laying down structure etc.) as well as by creating an ethos, an internal culture or a value system, of their own.

It also needs to be mentioned that an individual is as much a part of the global environment as an organisation is. He derives his own value system from this global environment. This value system is reflected in his attitudes towards work, his respect for the organisation's institutions and his compatibility with organisation's ethos. Thus, in the final analysis, values of the society permeate the values of the organisations and the values of the individual.

In the world of work, it has been found desirable to give to the organisation person 'the ability to move from one world of activity and the value system governing that to another world of activity and value system thereof'. In societies where several centuries lie telescoped in a miniaturised way, an individual may find his sheer travel through this way, demanding change of the concerns and issues to which he has to respond. Illustratively, in his ancestral home, he may have an agricultural ethos; in the Kasba or the provincial town, he may be living in an environment of extended village but when he reaches the metropolitan centre, it is a highly westernised world with an entirely different language and idiom. As a sales executive or a person charged with raising institutional funds, he deals with paradigms for action which perhaps would not be even fully understood by another member of his family, who has not worked through the different levels of iterations talked of in the foregoing example. This is indeed why management learnt through the writings of acknowledged signatories of western tradition or prestigious centres of management learning of the western variety have repeatedly to be interpreted and adapted to the real world conditions of another culture. All those, who have gone through it, acknowledge that this has often been a painful process and not all have measured up to it. Evidence of this is seen in the rate of turnover of the fresh entrants to an organisation and at times it is also seen in family tensions at a later point of time in the life cycle. Indeed on multiple occasions, a person from a joint family is perceived to have resources and expected to provide these resources for growth of the family, when in reality he may not even actually possess.

Modern organisations can hardly design work or the strategy of developing people without accounting for these factors, which alas never figure in the learning books of other cultures.

Organisation and the Environment

An organisation is a part of a larger continuum which is the society. Everything else in the society, other than the organisation itself, is the environment in the organisation. This includes the immediate environment or the 'task' environment which covers its customers, vendors, competitors, regulatory agencies, financial institutions etc. It also includes a wider environment which is comprised of the technology, culture and value system of the society.

An organisation continually interacts with its environment. In the General Systems Theory and Living Systems Theory perspective discussed in the next chapter in detail, an organisation as an open living system continually exchanges matter, energy and information with its environment. Through this process, it gains the property of negentropy (i.e. negative entropy) and thereby increases its orderliness or what can be termed as the degree of organisation. As an open living system, an organisation also has the property of 'dynamic homeostasis', which enables the organisation to maintain stability despite abnormal environmental disturbances. Finally, an organisation sets itself towards a process of growth through an optimum and appropriate mix of matter, energy and information inputs and outputs. In this process, it gradually assimilates parts of the environment, through successive stages of growth from one stable position to another, till it reaches its maximal limit of growth. While the process of growth is on, almost immediately is set in motion, in the organisation, a process of decay, which occurs primarily as a result of the competitive environmental pressures. The natural sequel to growth is therefore decay, which may take place gradually or at a faster pace, depending upon the net balance of the opposing forces of growth and decay.

What has been described above is a set of natural processes taking place in an organisation. These can however be greatly influenced by the 'management' dimension. Appropriate management interventions can facilitate growth and can help control decay. These also help in extending the period of smooth and effective organisational performance, a period in which the organisation is able to achieve its immediate goals, satisfy the needs of its organisational members and adapt itself to the environment.

Several managerial functions need to be performed for facilitating the process of growth and inhibiting the process of decay of organisation. The first and foremost function is what can be termed as 'boundary spanning'. This refers to the ability to scan the environment, pick up opportunities offered and meet the threat and challenges posed by the variety of events occurring and activities taking place in the environment. Obviously, this function is critical for the 'adaptability' of organisation with the environment. The second important function is to manage the organisation's internal environment. This requires an understanding of dynamics within the organisation resulting from the individual-organisation interface and skilled manipulation of this organisation dynamics. Both these kinds of managerial interventions are critical and, more often than not, are simultaneously required.

Organisations have to invest to maintain environmental goodwill. For instance, in several countries, where financial resources get routed excessively through a given agency or a set of agencies, organisations have been put in a position of meeting the needs of these changing agencies. This in turn has given leverage to personnel in the organisation, who take care of this interface in the internal decision making processes of the organisation. The distortion that this may cause on pristine principles of organisation management have very often been adversely commented upon. However, whether there is any commonality of laws and principles of determining the efficacy of managerial decision making, is a debate which remains to be resolved. The real world shows that like all organismic existence, organisations have adapted to the environment and left an impact on it.

Technology

The application of technology can be viewed as a kind of managerial intervention which helps enhance the adaptability of organisations to the environment. Technology, by definition, includes processes, techniques and innovations of all types based on scientific principles, which either enhance the productivity of operations or which help in production of better quality of goods and services. Thus, technology leads to economies of production. In fact, technology updation is crucial for organisational effectiveness.

However, technology can be a double edged weapon too. While it may bring in economics of scale, it may also constrain the nature and functionality of goods and services produced. The organisation may not remain market driven; it may become technology driven and the nature of technology application need not be necessarily compatible with the demands of the market. Thus, technology can have an unfavourable implication for the adaptability of the organisation with its environment.

Another way through which technology has an impact on organisational processes is through its property of dictating the work methods followed by the organisation. This also has implications on structure, on roles and responsibilities, on information flow and on decision/authority centres in the organisation. In fact, technology has its own sequence and compulsions which need to be reflected in the organisation structure.

Thus, technology has an overpowering influence on the organisation's internal environment, all of which may not necessarily be conducive to effective functioning of the organisation.

One often comes across terminologies like high tech and low tech, which by implication idolises high tech as noble, sophisticated and modern and denigrates low tech as old, unfashionable and unworthy. This philosophy is often exaggerated to the point of what may be termed as 'ridicul-tech'. However, high or low technology is a relative concept; what is important is that the technology should be appropriate to the needs of the organisation, which are dictated by its needs for adaptability with the environment.

For understanding the functioning of an organisation, it is perhaps just as important to understand the technology used by the organisation for its operations (whether manufacturing of service) or for managerial decision making. This will be an important determinant of the ability of a manager to successfully and intelligently utilise the strengths provided by the technology.

Organisation's Culture

An organisation is not a mechanistic system but an organic entity. Like any organic entity, it not only carries out the processes of matter, energy and information exchange, but also processes an inner core of beliefs and values, shared by organisational members. Culture of the organisation "is the product of the general pattern of behaviour, shared beliefs and values". Organisation's culture is like myths of society, which impart it a sense of dynamism, without its culture, an organisation is a soulless entity.

Where does the organisational culture come from? The answer to this question lies again in the adaptability argument. The culture of the organisation is a response to the objective values of the outside environment. However, it does not imply that organisational culture has to be a replica of the environmental culture.

On the other hand, the deterioration in environmental culture may actually necessitate and warrant organisational culture, different from it. For instance, when inefficiency abounds almost universally, an organisation with efficiency criteria on the top of its value system, is likely to be needed most and is expected to survive and grow.

It is clear that the society, individual and the organisation get into a symbiotic linkage. It becomes incumbent upon the organisation to carry out the induction of the individual in a manner such that the culture 'off the job' does not influence culture 'of the job' in any dysfunctional way. Briefing, induction training and monitoring are some of the instruments used to achieve this. The question, however, remains a tricky one. This has very often required the inputs of management art rather than management science.

Socio-Technical Systems

We have discussed about technology and culture separately in the context of individual-organisation-environment interface. However, they are not necessarily separable concepts. In fact, technology has a profound impact on organisational culture, since by its technical compulsions, it also forces a particular set of value systems to take preference over others. Similarly, organisational culture may be a dominant factor in selecting the technology to be inducted into the organisation. Though, technology selection is a result of logical analysis, the domain of logical analysis lies with people embedded in a specific organisational culture, which implicitly becomes a determinant of technology selection.

It is also apparent that technology cannot be allowed to override individual's expectations from the organisations. If in the name of productivity, technology dominates upon or conflicts with the social aspects of organisational life, it will soon become a source of organisation's degeneration. It is, therefore, necessary to develop mutually compatible social and technical subsystems. A harmonious blending of the two is necessary to ensure that organisational effectiveness is achieved in all its dimensions.

Concluding Comments

Wheels within wheels within wheels, that is how we described the individual-organisation-environment interface in the beginning of this chapter. However, there is something more to this syndrome of wheels which lies at its hub. This is what we may call the organisation's views or models, which provide differing perspectives on why organisations behave as they behave. This is the subject matter of the next chapter.

Chapter 3

Emergence of Organisation Theories

Organisations are like kaleidoscopes; different configurations of the same elements can be seen by taking different positions. The academicians, the management practitioners and organisation researchers have all been viewing the organisations ever since these became a subject of study and have been formulating organisation theories on the basis of what they see in this organisational kaleidoscope. This has led to the evolution of several organisation theories, especially in the twentieth century, which have subsequently been categorised according to their key focus. In this chapter, some of these theories have been explored in a greater detail.

The Classical Organisation Theories

There are three major organisational theories of the early twentieth century which have been categorised as classical organisation theories. These are Fredrick W. Taylor's Scientific Management, Max Weber's Bureaucracy and Henry Fayol's Principles of General and Administrative Management.

Fredrick Taylor: The Scientific Management

Perhaps, the earliest documented theory of organisations is that propounded by Fredrick Taylor in the year 1900 and termed it as Scientific Management. This was one of the earliest systematic attempts to view the functioning of organisations and suggest ways and means to improve their efficiency and productivity. Taylor concluded that the typical areas of improvement in the organisations included the work methods adopted, the wage system, the supervision pattern and the system for recruitment and training. Accordingly, he surmised that the work methods need to be analysed in detail and improved work methods need to be established on the basis of time and motion studies. Obviously, his argument related to production area, though in principle, what he said is equally applicable to non-production areas.

Taylor also propagated the idea of incentive schemes to reward those employees who contributed more to the production output. This kind of differential payment system, in his opinion, was necessary in ensuring that the overall performance of the organisation improved. Another interesting concept given by Taylor emphasized segregation of supervision function in the organisation on the basis of functional specialisation. For instance, he advocated that the quality supervision should be distinct from production supervision. Last, but not least, Taylor stressed upon the need to have scientific system of recruitment and training of workmen.

In essence, Taylor's key propositions of organisation theory appear to be the following:

(a) There is one best way of doing a job and the organisation should strive to find out the best way.
(b) Financial incentives steer the performance of workers and thus help in improving overall efficiency.
(c) The supervision of jobs is required to be organised in a professional manner on the basis of specialisation of knowledge.
(d) In order to ensure that there is a right worker for every job, the selection and training of workers has to be carefully carried out.

There has been severe criticism of Taylor's Scientific Management approach on the grounds that it is highly task oriented and is not concerned at all with the behavioural aspects of human beings in the organisation. However, much of the criticism, in retrospective, appears to be exaggerated. It is worthwhile quoting Koontz, O'Donnel and Weihrich in this context:

"The principal concern of Taylor's Scientific Management School is to increase efficiency in production, not only to lower costs and raise profits, but also to make possible, increased pay for workers. The principles of scientific management are:

(a) Replacing rules of thumb with science (organised knowledge).
(b) Obtaining harmony in group action, rather than discord.
(c) Achieving co-operation of human beings rather than chaotic individualism.
(d) Working for maximum output rather than restricted output.
(e) Developing all workers to the fullest extent possible for their own and their company's highest prosperity."

Notwithstanding the criticisms, Taylor's scientific management is one of the first important milestones in the evolution of organisation theory.

Max Weber and Bureaucracy

Bureaucracy as a form of organisation and principles related to effective functioning of "bureaucratic" organisations were propounded by Max Weber, a German organisation theorist during 1909. This form of organisation is most suited to non-profit, non-competitive organisations such as government organisations. The principles of bureaucracy ensure that organisations of this kind function in an objective and unbiased manner. The key principles of bureaucracy are the following:

(a) Insistence on following Standard Rules

An organisation should formulate standard rules which will be applied to all persons irrespective of their position and nature of work. These persons may be suppliers, customers or employees of the organisation.

(b) Systematic Division of Work

The work allocation amongst various employees should be carried out systematically and explicitly defined so that there are no overlaps.

(c) Principle of Hierarchy

The work should be so divided that it flows from one level of hierarchy to the next and so on, with each level adding value commensurate with its authority and competence.

(d) Knowledge of and Training in the Application of Rules

The employees should be fully aware of the standard rules being followed in the organisation and their implications. They should be provided training in the application of these rules.

(e) Recording in Writing of Administrative Acts, Decisions and Rules

To ensure that there is a clear and common understanding of the rules and that there is a complete transparency in their application, all administrative Acts, decisions and rules should be recorded in writing.

(f) Rational Personnel Administration

There should be sound personnel policies in the organisation, especially with regard to recruitment (to be based on merits) remuneration (to be based on position in the hierarchy) and promotions (to be systematic and equitable to all employees). The values of loyalty and commitment to the organisation should be nourished.

The above mentioned principles of bureaucracy apparently provide a very pragmatic approach to the design and functioning of organisations. However, in actual practice, bureaucracies have been observed to be procedure oriented rather than result oriented and thus are seen to be grossly inefficient. Nevertheless, the main appeal of the principles of bureaucracy is the sense of fair play and equity evoked by them. Perhaps, the time when Max Weber propounded these principles demanded them owing to exploitative situations taking place in the then organisations. As such, Max Weber's contribution to the evolution of organisation theory is a significant milestone.

Henry Fayol and Principles of General Management

Henry Fayol, a French Management practitioner, is credited with propounding principles of general and industrial management based on his vast experience of managing organisations. In his book "Administrative Industrielle et Generale" published in French in 1916, Henry Fayol narrated 14 such principles, which are by no means exhaustive. These are as follows:

1. **Division of Work:** The work to be carried out in an organisation needs to be allocated to people on the basis of their specialisation.
2. **Authority and Responsibility:** Each person in an organisation should have his responsibility well defined to enable him discourage his responsibility, each person would require a commensurate authority.
3. **Discipline:** An organisation will be able to perform well only if it is ensured that there is obedience to authority.
4. **Unity of Command:** There should be only one person to whom a subordinate should report. This is necessary for avoiding confusion and for helping to pinpoint responsibility.
5. **Unity of Direction:** There should be as complete an agreement as possible amongst individual and organisational objectives so that there is no dissipation of organisational energy for purposes which have no relevance for the organisation.
6. **Subordination of Individual Interest to General Interest:** If a situation arises in which there is a conflict between the interests of the organisation and an individual, it is essential that organisational interest is given precedence over individual's interest.
7. **Remuneration:** The remuneration to be given to the employees should be judiciously determined based on

factors such as practices followed in the industry, profitability of the organisation, cost of living and nature of job performed.

8. **Centralization vs. Decentralization:** The extent of centralisation (or decentralisation) in the organisation should be such that the organisation functions most effectively. This has to be determined on the basis of nature of business, size and resources available.
9. **Scalar Chain:** The exercise of authority in the organisation should normally be done, from a senior to a subordinate through the scalar chain that connects them. Only in exceptional cases, this scalar chain should be short-circuited.
10. **Order**: It is essential that there is an orderliness in the organisation. This orderliness is manifested in the form of orderly work flows, scientific selection, correct work allocations etc.
11. **Equity:** The organisation should be equitable towards all employees in terms of authority and responsibility, remuneration, career paths etc.
12. **Stability of Tenure of Personnel**: All employees should have a stability of tenure in the organisation.
13. **Initiative:** The initiative amongst employees in the organisation should be encouraged through a conducive work environment.
14. **Espirit de Corps:** Team spirit amongst employees of an organisation should be consciously built-up and sustained.

It can be observed that almost all these principles have a universal appeal. Anyone who works in an organisation will vouch for the sanctity of these principles, since many of our day-to-day experiences in organisation support one or the other of these principles. In this respect, Henry Fayol has made a singular contribution to organisation theory.

However, the main criticisms of Henry Fayol's principles are that these have not been empirically tested, and have been stated as unconditional statements, as if applicable in all organisational situations. Besides, one can find contradictions between a few principles; for instance, division of work on the basis of specialisation often necessitates that the principle of unity of command is flouted, by having multiple reporting relationships.

Comments on Classical Organisation Theories

A close look at the various classical organisation theories briefly presented above indicates that they are all characterised by task orientation and are primarily concerned with improvement in efficiency and productivity through scientific organisation of work and optimum resource allocation. The key concerns of these theories centre around work flows, division of labour, authority, span of control, etc. Though it may be erroneous to say than these theories are not concerned with the needs and expectations of human beings in the organisations, it is true that these theories consider human beings easily adaptable to various rules and principles dictated by best ways of organising work. However, it became clear during early years of organisational analysis that human beings cannot be taken for granted and that any principles of management devoid of an understanding of human behaviour cannot be expected to satisfactorily explain organisation functioning.

The Behavioural Theories of Organisations

Rightly or wrongly, the classical organisation theories were criticised on the ground that they ignored the human being. The concern for human being, therefore, became the focal point of many a theory that followed. The pioneering work in this regard was carried out by Elton Mayo through his famous Hawthrone experiments in the year 1927. A brief description follows:

Elton Mayo: The Hawthrone Experiments

These experiments were conducted at the Hawthrone plant of Western Electric Company to empirically examine the impact of changes in the degree of illumination and other factors related to work environment on the productivity of workers. Four experiments were conducted in succession; these were the illumination experiment, the relay assembly test room experiment, the interviewing programme and the bank wiring observation room.

In the illumination experiment, the production of workers was measured at various levels of illumination. It was observed that production increased when the level of illumination was increased; but surprisingly the production also increased when the level of illumination was decreased. This suggested that the real reason for increase in production was not really the illumination but some other factor.

In the relay assembly test room experiment, a group of women workers were asked to work for varying lengths of working days and rest pauses and other physical conditions and their production measured. There was no direct supervision of the group during the period of experimentation. It was observed that irrespective of the changes in the working condition, the production kept on increasing and stabilised at a higher level, even when all changes were discontinued. This led to the inference that the increase in production was the result of a belief amongst the group that they were cared for by the company. This motivated them and boosted their sense of commitment.

In the third experiment, over 20,000 workers were interviewed with a view to obtain their perceptions on the impact of type of supervision, working conditions, etc. These interviews indicated that the formation of informal work groups was instrumental in formulating their attitudes and behaviour which, in turn influenced their output.

In the final experiment, a group of 14 workers was subjected to continual observations over a period of time to determine the impact of financial incentives *vis-à-vis* informal group norms on productivity. These observations revealed that the informal group norms were far more influential in determining the productivity levels achieved by the group, as compared to the financial incentives.

Thus, the Hawthrone experiments led to the emergence of the human relations school/theory of organisations.

According to this theory, the concern for employees welfare can be a very important factor for improving their productivity. The theory also emphasises the significance of informal work groups as a source of influence on productivity of employees. The needs for motivation of employees and increased group cohesiveness through effective leadership are also highlighted.

Further Developments in Human Relation Theory

Apart from Elton Mayo, there were several other contributors to the human relations theory. For instance, the works of Maslow (Hierarchy of Needs), Douglas McGregor (Theory X and Theory Y), Hertzberg (Hygiene and Maintenance Factors Theory) and Vroom (Expectancy Theory) have made significant contributions to further develop this theory. Some of these contributions have been discussed again in Chapter 6.

The emergence of industrial psychology and personnel management were two more notable developments with regard to the human relations theory. Industrial psychology is concerned with understanding the behaviour of individuals in the organisational settings and employing this understanding to improve the match between individuals and the organisations. Similarly, the establishment of personnel management departments in the organisations became a reflection of the growing realisation that attention towards employee welfare is crucial for organisational effectiveness.

The human relations school/theory hypothesises that people want to belong and to be recognised as individuals. The manager's basic task is to make each worker feel useful and important; he should keep his subordinates informed and listen to their observations on his plans. He should allow his subordinates to exercise some self-direction and self-control on routine matters. The sharing of information with subordinates and involving them in routine decisions will satisfy their basic needs to belong and to feel important. Satisfying these needs will improve morale and reduce resistance to formal authority and subordinates will willingly co-operate.

There is always a danger of practising the beliefs of human relations school to a ridiculous level. An example of this is offered by a manager in a small organisation who frequently joked and laughed with his employees. He often patted them on the back; hosted frequent and expensive parties; supplemented income of certain favoured employees with paid-for trips and vacations. He resolved conflicts by avoiding issues and attempting to laugh it off. He rewarded even the incompetent employees with token and merit salary increases. The net result of his behaviour was a relatively happy but stagnant organisation.

The Social Systems Theories of Organisations

The behavioural theories of organisation, especially the human relations school, with their excessive focus on the human being, perhaps missed the fact that organisations need to be looked at in totality rather than merely from the point of view of human relations. From this consciousness emerged the social systems school, which emphasises the relationship of parts to the whole in an organisation.

The central theme of the Social System School/Theories of organisations is that whatever affects one part of the organisational system also affects other parts. When the organisation is viewed as a social system, questions of structural and human variables assume new importance. No longer can the job functions of a machine be divorced from the successful functioning of the entire organisation. Nor can the morale of one employee be a minor concern. No longer can a single message sent through a grapevine be ignored nor can the orders of one supervisor to his staff be minimised. Questions of job design, line of command, span of control and decision making are equal in importance as the questions of attitude, morale, behaviour, role and personality.

The evolution of the social systems school can be traced to the contributions of Chester Bernard and Eris Trist. These are briefly described below.

Chester Bernard: The Cooperative Systems

Chester Bernard propounded the cooperative systems theory in

1938. According to this theory, the need for cooperation arises owing to the basic physical and biological limitations of the individuals. This leads to the establishment of cooperative systems or organisations, the continuance of which depends upon the effectiveness of the cooperative effort amongst individuals.

The cooperative system theory recognised the existence of both formal and informal organisations and their need for ensuring effective cooperation. The need for interactions, formal and informal, amongst the members is also recognised in this theory.

The concept of cooperative systems was elaborated by Chester Bernard in his book "Functions of the Executive". According to him, the 'executive' in the organisation has to perform the functions of maintaining communication within the organisation, securing of essential services from the individuals and formulating and defining purpose. It is the executive's responsibility to "integrate the whole" by finding the best balance amongst all these needs.

In the cooperative system theory of Chester Bernard one can see a recognition of the inevitability of considering the social system of organisations for ensuring organisational effectiveness.

Eric Trist: Socio-Technical Systems Approach

The socio-technical systems approach was propounded by Eric Trist of Tavistock Institute in England in 1951. Through his studies on production problems in coal mining, Eric Trist concluded that the social and technical subsystems of an organisation cannot be separated from each other. They have to be designed simultaneously, keeping in view the unique requirements of each other. The technical subsystem significantly affects several attributes of the social system such as group behaviour of organisation members.

The socio-technical system approach was also an important milestone in the development of organisation theory, since it brought out a new paradigm for designing and improving the functioning of organisations.

The Systems Theories of Organisations

The systems theories of organisations had their origins in the social systems approach. However, these developed into explicit theories with the development of 'Systems' concepts during the fifties. Some of the organisation theories which evolved from these basic systems concepts include Bertanalffy's General Systems Theory framework, Stafford Beer's Viable Systems Model and James Miller's Living Systems Theory. While these theories are discussed in the ensuing paragraphs, it is worthwhile dwelling upon the basic systems concepts, as below.

A system is a set of parts together with relationships between the parts and their attributers. Through the process of creation of a system, new properties emerge, which do not exist at the part stage but come into being with the creation of a system. A system may be open or closed. An open system exchanges matter, energy and information with environment and thereby increases its degree of orderliness. A closed system on the other hand, does not exchange matter, energy or information with the environment. An open system maintains dynamic homeostasis, a property which enables it to remain stable in the face of abnormal external disturbances.

Bertanalffy: The General Systems Theory of Organisations

The General Systems Theory framework propounded by Bertanalffy is based on the premise that there are many similarities in the basic properties governing behaviour and performance of diverse types of systems and, therefore, natural laws of organisation govern systems at all levels of existence. Since, organisations are also systems of a kind, they are also governed by such common laws.

Russel L. Ackoff and Mark Braham have contributed to the development of an organisation theory based on the above approach. Organisations as per this theory, can be deemed to be special kind of systems, which have the following characteristics:

(a) Some of the components are living beings ('animals' as stated by Ackoff).

(b) Responsibility for choice among the sets of possible acts in any specific situation is divided among two or more individuals or groups of individuals.
(c) The functionally distinct subgroups are aware of each other's behaviour either through communication or observation.
(d) The system has some freedom of choice of both means and ends.
(e) Organisations have specific purposes, objectives and goals for which they have been created.
(f) They possess a structural or hierarchical order.
(g) They have decision making procedures either implicitly given or explicitly stated.
(h) They grow and decay with time.
(i) They compete with other organisations in terms of exchange of matter, energy and information with the environment and endeavour to retain their wholeness and identity at all times.

The above elaboration of an organisation systems provides an interesting conceptual understanding of organisations. However, it only goes a certain distance in helping one identifying methods of increasing organisational effectiveness.

To round off the picture in the paragraphs that follow a brief elaboration is made to the living system theory of organisations; management cybernetic model of an organisation; the political view of organisations and the economics view.

The Living Systems Theory of Organisations

The Living Systems Theory propounded by James Miller considers organisations as a type of what he calls living systems. He identifies living systems as those which have significant inputs, throughputs and outputs of various kinds of matter, energy and information. Parts of the living systems are instituted from life giving substance. The theory identifies seven hierarchical levels of living system, namely a cell, an organ, an organism, a group, an organisation, a society and a super-national system. These levels differ from each other in their degree of complexity and the nature of emergent properties. Apparently, organisations are at a fairly high hierarchical level.

As per the living systems theory, there exists nineteen critical subsystems whose processes are essential to life. These may be categorised into three groups, namely subsystems processing matter, energy and information; subsystems processing matter and energy; and subsystems processing information. Out of these, 'decider' subsystem is the most important, since it controls the entire living system. (A detailed discussion of the 19 critical subsystems is far from the purview of this book).

An organisation as a living system may become pathological if there is an inadequacy or excess of matter energy inputs or if there are inputs of inappropriate forms of matter and energy. Other reasons for pathological behaviour of an organisation may be inadequate inputs or an information overload. Inputs or mal-adapting genetic information may be yet another source of pathology.

The Living System Theory provides a useful diagnostic method for identifying problems with an organisation. For this purpose, the existing organisational scenario is required to be mapped on the 19 critical subsystems and then the lacunae be identified based on an analysis of how these subsystems appear to be functioning.

Management Cybernetic Model of an Organisation

Stafford Beer has developed a systems model of an organisation, based upon the fundamental concepts of cybernetics, 'The science of communications and control in the biological, man-machine social system.' This model has been developed by identifying necessary and sufficient conditions for a viable system and viability has been defined as the ability to maintain a separate existence.

The model identifies five subsystems of an organisation. System 1 is a set of operational subsystems or divisions of the organisation. System 2 is the co-ordination subsystem whose function is to ensure that various operational divisions act in harmony. System 3 is the control subsystem aimed at maintaining internal stability of the organisation. System 4 is the intelligence subsystem responsible for planning and development functions. System 5 is the policy subsystem for developing policy and for balancing the internal and external demands placed on the organisation by systems 3 and 4, respectively.

The model also incorporates the concept of variety engineering. Variety implies to the degree of complexity of an entity and is an indicator of its ability to match the pressures faced by it from other entities. As per the concept of variety engineering, the management of an operational unit increases its variety and decreases, the variety of the operational unit by using variety amplifiers and variety attenuators respectively, thereby matching their varieties. These amplifiers and attenuators are specific organisational interaction and information filtering mechanisms, respectively. For instance, increased departmentalisation will increase the variety of the operational units.

The viable system model also provides a very useful diagnostic method to analyse organisational problems. Mapping of the existing organisation on different subsystems of the viable system model helps identify the sources of lacunae in organisational functioning and suggests remedial actions.

The Contingency Theory of Organizations

The simplest way to describe the contingency theory is to say: "it depends" and "there is no best way". In other words, what form will be taken by an organization's structure and processes, is the outcome of and is contingent upon a variety of factors. These factors are embedded into the external environment of the organization and may include political, economic, social, technological, ecological or legal issues which the organization has to deal with. As these issues bring in elements of uncertainty, the organization copes with these by appropriately designing its structure and processes. In fact, different subsystems of a large organization may be confronting different environmental issues and accordingly may require different structural and process configurations to deal with their different local challenges. Thus, contingency is a source of uncertainty emanating from the external environment of the organization and the organization must configure its internal structure to address these contingencies. The key messages of the contingency theory are that there is no single best way to organize; that all ways of organizing are not equally effective in dealing with the environment; and that the external environmental factors influence the way an organization structures itself.

The origins of contingency theory date back to the 1960s and credit is given to several authors for propounding this theory. The prominent among them are Tom Burns & G.M. Stalker (1961) and Paul Lawrence & Jay Lorsch (1967). Studies by Burns and Stalker in the U.K. among textile mills and electronics manufacturers concluded that companies with "organic" structure were more effective in unstable, changing environments, whereas companies with "mechanistic" structure fared well in relatively stable and less uncertain environments. The relatively stable and less uncertain environments were characterized by having greater need for routine and unchanging tasks, for which efficiency, high degree of specialization and elaborate procedures were important. This was possible through greater formalization and centralization. However, the relatively unstable and rapidly changing environments warranted tasks that were non-routine and which required low job specialization, greater creativity and lesser reliance on rules and procedures. This was possible through lesser formalization and higher degree of decentralization.

Studies by Lawrence and Lorsch were conducted in the USA in the plastics, food processing and the container manufacturing industry to determine how different departments in these industries respond to the environmental factors by adopting different structures. These studies revealed that among organizations in the plastics industry, considered as relatively less stable than the other two, organizations adopted less formalized, open and decentralized structures; and both departmental differentiation and cross-functional integration were high. In contrast, among the organizations in the container manufacturing industry, considered as relatively more stable, the organizations relied more on centralized and formalized structures, and both departmental differentiation and cross-functional integration were low. The organizations in the food processing industry, which stood in between the other two in terms of perceived stability and degree of environmental uncertainty, fared moderately with regard to the degree of formalization in the structural forms adopted and the extent of both departmental differentiation and cross-functional integration.

Another way of looking at the contingency theory is that environmental factors are important since they influence the ability of an organization to obtain resources. Since resources are critical in performing organizational functions, each organization has to actively endeavour for a set of mutually compatible structure and processes which enhance its ability to acquire the desired resources. This view of the organization is also referred to as the resource dependence theory. It postulates that the goal of an organization is to minimize its dependence on other organizations for supply of scarce resources; and to achieve this, the organization adopts most appropriate structural forms.

An interesting aspect of the contingency theory is that the evolution of structure and processes can be highly dynamic in nature. As environments become increasingly complex and fast-paced, the imperative of dynamically changing the ways of managing an organization creates its own demand for relatively flexible structures and processes. The stability associated with traditional organizations gives way to rapidly changing configurations adapting to the external and internal environmental triggers. In a sense, the contingency theory is also a reflection of the open systems view of an organization. Just as an open system continually interfaces with its environment, in the same way, an organization too continually and iteratively responds to the environmental factors, both from within and those external to it. One can also argue that the role of management according to the contingency theory is to continually seek a dynamic alignment between an organization and its environment. A certain degree of proactive approach on the part of management in achieving the requisite fit with the external and internal environmental factors is expected in the contingency approach.

One important aspect of the contingency theory in the modern day organization is the influence of information technology as a dominant environmental factor influencing the organization structures and processes. The information technology applications in business can be seen to dictate the way work is allocated, decision making rights are distributed and reporting relationships emerge in organizations. One way to look at this is what can be called 'technological determinism', which, simply stated, means that the technology determines the form taken by organizational structure and processes. A more moderate view, however, is that IT has an inherent flexibility, and it can support whichever form is taken by the organization structures and processes.

The greatest weakness of the contingency theory is that it fails to provide any clear-cut universally applicable principles to determine the appropriate organizational forms that a company should take, since each company can be seen to be in a unique position with regard to the external environmental factors faced by it. Secondly, just because the organization choses certain structural forms considering the environmental factors facing it, there is no guarantee that the chosen form is indeed the best fit for the organization. However, contingency theory has its uses too. For example, it helps managers get rid of artificial constraints to the possible solutions they must adopt for dealing with external environment challenges, as there are no best ways prescribed to them.

The 'Political' View of Organisations

Organisations have been seen as excellent examples of political entities by several organisational theorists. As per this view, organisations are inherently political in nature and organisational members are continually engaged in the quest for power. In this model, the reason deterre of organisations appears to be essentially political. This view supports the belief that organisations themselves do not have any goals. However, their participants, have their individual goals, as well as, perceived goals for the organisations.

The Economic View of Organisations

In the economic view of organisations, organisations exist because market transactions can be handled more efficiently and economically with the help of organisations as against through competing entities in the free market. The Agency theory of an organisation, for instance, deems an organisation as an agency relationship, built on a set of contracts among self-interested agents. As a consequence, when decision making authority is delegated to agents, it cannot be guaranteed that the decisions will be aligned with the interests of the principal. The divergence of interests between the principal and agents can breed numerous problems. Agency theory tries to explain how an organisation can remain viable in spite of these problems.

Another theory in the economic doctrine is the transaction cost economic perspective. This starts by looking at problems in using a market and considers organisation as a solution to these problems. This theory recognises that the operation of a market is not costless and that it is important to assess transaction costs in the analysis of economic activity. According to this theory, the organisation is a substitute for market mechanism, created to reduce transaction costs.

Concluding Comments

It is useful to remind oneself that organisations can mean different things to different people, depending upon their perception by people. The differing perspectives provide very useful and relevant conclusions about how organisations perform as they perform. However, none of them provide a complete understanding of organisation. If at all they achieve something, it is the realisation that there are problems in understanding organisations, often complicated, when simultaneously differing perspectives are employed and solutions to observed problems arrived at using these differing perspectives. To be true, organisations defy understanding, despite plethora of organisational theories and models.

Chapter 4

Nature and Dynamics of Organisation Structures

A question often posed in organisation theory is whether organisations can exist without structure. It may be tempting to answer 'yes' to this question in the wake of the emerging trends of flat organisations, networked organisations, matrix organisations and the like. However, the fact is that even the above innovations are related to the structure. They do not negate the structure of the organisation, they, on the other hand, modify the structure from conventional perceptions to unconventional forms.

Structure is as fundamental as an organisation. It is in fact the essence of the organisation. The structure provides an organisation capabilities to perform all tasks which are essential for its sustenance. It provides the organisation a mechanism to generate a large variety of responses required to meet the challenges posed by environment.

A structure comes into being by the sheer process of formation of the organisation. It exists without a conscious designing. However, a careful designing of the structure will go a long way in achieving organisational effectiveness. The structure evolves over time; this evolution may be dictated by environmental pressures or may merely be a response to the power struggle within the organisation. The structural change may also be a discontinuous one, rather than being evolutionary, particularly when a significant change takes place in the policy variables of the organisation. For instance, introduction of new technology, new products, changes in ownership or top management etc. may necessitate discreet structural change. In any case, structure is not a static entity, it is a dynamic manifestation of conscious or unconscious strategic changes in the thinking about how the organisation should function to remain in tune with the demands posed by its internal and external environment.

Though, organisation structure has not been defined in this book as yet, some clues to its definition have however appeared by now. It is often understood that structure is the depiction of formal reporting relationships amongst organisational members on a chart. However, this is an incomplete and rather inaccurate understanding of the structure. To put it more comprehensively, structure is the sum total of various permanent and/or relatively more enduring arrangements made jointly by the organisational members for carrying out all the necessary functions required by the organisation. It is a mix of designated roles and responsibilities, accountabilities, delegations of authority, work allocation and division, rules and regulations, information flow mechanisms amongst members and methods of evaluating performance. It includes several formal systems introduced in the organisation to provide guidelines for promoting optimum work methods. For instance, departmentalisation, setting of procedures manuals, and control systems represent different aspects of structures of organisations.

It may help to give a concrete analogy to what structures do to organisation. Look at a building being built or knocked down. One will find beams, iron rods and gratings. That is the permanent structure of that building. Look at the human body; the structure comes out of the skeleton. All organisations have their structures. They are dependent on the product/service line, basis technology built into the system and the assumptions at the time the organisation was brought into existence. All changes which take place in the organisation will have to account for this given situation. Whereas, theoretically it is possible to change the basic structure of an organisation, like a broken marriage it can be both costly and painful. An appreciation of this fact will help a decision maker to distinguish between that part of the organisation structure which, to be altered, requires a fundamental change and that part of the structure, which can easily be changed without heavy costs or fundamental change. To point towards this difference is not to discourage change but to create an awareness of the art of the possible. It is to show that change like *status quo* has a price tag to it.

Like all analogies, the above analogy to a human body and a building is a limited one. The critical issues of organisation structure remain distribution of roles, putting together of the tasks, design of jobs and working out their relationships. It helps to reduce wild fluctuations of individual preferences. It helps to define decision making roles and provides a channel of information flow. One of the inherent outcomes is the emergence of a hierarchy. The current debate in organisation management is related to the levels of hierarchy which is optimal to the organisation.

Hierarchies in Organisations

Hierarchies are the most important and obvious manifestations of organisation structures. Hierarchies emerge primarily from the fact that work cannot be performed by one individual alone and needs to be shared in accordance with competence/skills and volume which can be handled by individuals. The mere fact that a given work is being performed by more than one organisation member gives rise to more work of a different kind—that of planning, co-ordinating, monitoring, appraising, controlling, motivating etc.—in other words, managerial functions. These managerial functions are again required at higher level, to plan, monitor and control the functions of a number of managers at a given level. In many situations, the various managerial functions are also required to be segregated into the roles and responsibilities of different persons, since specialised inputs are required for some or all of them. Thus, one sees the emergence of different hierarchical level in the organisation structure.

Another view of the emergence of different hierarchical levels is provided by the reference to 'the process of organisation growth'. This process comprises of 'differentiation', i.e. development of organisational units which perform specialised functions and 'integration', i.e. assignment of functions which are integrated in nature, which aim at providing cohesiveness in nature. The differentiation and integration processes together result in organisation growth in successive stages, adding new hierarchical levels at each stage of growth.

There is no simple answer to this question of how many hierarchical levels an organisation should have, since it is an organisation specific issue. However, it is clear that if there are a large number of hierarchical levels, decision making becomes more and more difficult since the information flow in the organisation, whether upwards or downwards, will tend to be delayed and skewed.

Often hierarchies are created not because they are functionally required but because they provide a venue for pushing unwanted people up in the organisation or for providing promotional avenue. These dysfunctional hierarchies are in fact the cause for reduced organisational effectiveness.

Flat organisations are the ones which have virtually no hierarchy. All organisational members perform diverse but specific functions and are co-ordinated at an apex level by the chief executive. The information flow from each organisational member to the chief executive is so comprehensive that he is in a position to control all operations without assistance of any middle management levels. However, the concept of flat organisations, despite its appeal is more utopian than real, at least as on date. Perhaps, in a future period, advents in information technology will make flat organisation more feasible than at present.

Span of Control

The concept of span of control is closely related to that of hierarchy. At any given position, a manager has several number of persons directly reporting to him, constituting his span of control. More the number of persons reporting to a position, more is the span of control for the position. Obviously, for a flat organisation, the span of control is very large. On the other hand, an organisation with a large number of levels of hierarchy is expected to have shorter spans of control at various levels, though it need not necessarily be so.

It is expected that when a number of persons (forming the span of control) are reporting to a given position, the manager holding that position exercises a 'unity of command', i.e. all these persons follow his direction and are controlled solely by him. However, in real life situation, unity of command is a myth. More often than not, there is someone else, somewhere else in the organisation, who directs and controls the functioning of some or all of these persons; this is dictated by the needs of the organisation.

Again, there is no simple answer to this question of what constitutes an optimum span of control. The span of control at different levels can be different, depending upon the nature of functions being co-ordinated or controlled by the person whose span of control is to be determined. If the subordinates are carrying out diverse independent types of functions, the span of control may be higher, than if they were carrying out interrelated tasks requiring frequent co-ordination and intervention from the senior. On the other hand, if the nature of subordinates functions is similar and is at an operating level, it may be possible to have a larger span of control.

The span of control is also a function of the effectiveness of communications in the organisation. A higher span of control is sustainable by an organisation if the information flow to the manager on the work being performed is unambigious and timely, providing him the capability of effective monitoring and control of a larger number of persons. However, if there are constraints in flow of information, it may not be possible to smoothly handle a larger span of control.

Location provides another dimension to the question of the possible span of control for a manager and is linked with the issue of communications and information flow in the organisation. Obviously, if the subordinates are located close to the manager at the same location (e.g. in the same building), or in the same city, there can be larger span of control, because of good communication amongst them; however, if some of the subordinates are located in different cities or countries, communication, despite availability of technology, may not be as good as that which can sustain a higher span of control. On the other hand, advent of modern information technology has made it easier to have multi-location span of control.

Line and Staff Functions

Hierarchy presupposes a unity of command, which presupposes that the manager is capable of planning, executing, monitoring and controlling every task or function being performed by his subordinates covered by his span of control. Perhaps, it is possible when the organisation is well defined and stable; the nature of technology, being used in the organisation is simple and the manager can in a short time-frame acquire adequate knowledge of all that he is managing. However, in today's organisations, these issues are far more complex, and to expect a person to possess all the capabilities is too much. Even if theoretically it were possible for a person to possess all such capabilities, the high degree of specialisation required and the effort necessary to make use of the specialised knowledge and update the same, will warrant that many of these functions are performed by a specialist. For example, industrial engineering support to a production manager may be provided by a dedicated individual or group of individual engineers. Such specialist functions providing professional support to a manager can be deemed as staff functions and the manager with the regular hierarchy and span of control, can be deemed to be the line manager.

A staff function is essentially an advisory function. It does not exercise authority over the functioning of the manager or his subordinates. The advice rendered by the person holding staff position may be accepted or rejected at the discretion of the line manager. However, the staff position carries with it the authority of knowledge. The support of top management also provides a weightage to a staff positions' views. It is thus likely that in real life situation, a staff position may exert more influence than the line manager.

The staff function itself may be performed by a group of experts rather than a single individual. This again will require organising the activities of such an expert group, possibly through a hierarchy, thus taking the form of a line function within a staff function. Interestingly, this may further extend into a staff function within the staff function. At some stage, the terminology of line and staff becomes totally irrelevant. In fact, organisations seldom designate functions as line or staff and the practice in real life situation, in fact, helps to differentiate between line functions and staff functions.

Information Systems for Management

Information flow in an organisation is a vital process influencing the nature and dynamics of organisation structures. Information is the thread which binds the organisation together; it is the entity which brings in a degree of cohesiveness in the organisation. Whether or not an information system is designed for management, information flow always exists. There may be a high degree of oral communication (interpersonal or through telephone) or written communication (through memos) or a combination of both. There may be formal or informal modes of information flow. There may be a grapevine, spreading information (or perhaps misinformation) faster than the formal channels. It is only through all such information flows within the organisation, however, that organisation structures gain their dynamism.

Information systems for management of Management Information System (MIS) as it is most commonly called refers to a well designed system of acquiring, generating and disseminating information to various levels of management to enable them perform decision making functions. These decision making functions may be at policy level, strategy level or operational level and may relate to structured or non-structured decisions.

The design of MIS is a specialised function. It involves obtaining a clear insight into the objectives of the organisation, identifying its critical success factors and the corresponding information needs and, on the basis of the same, preparing detailed design of the reports which will be submitted to various levels of management on periodic basis identifying the source documents using which the information reports will be generated and specify the organisational arrangements for implementation of the MIS. Often design of MIS also implies designing a computerised system and, therefore, involves determination of hardware and software needs and other aspects related to computerisation. The business technology, organisation size and the number of locations where its subunits are situated influence the nature of MIS for the organisation.

Information systems themselves are dynamic. The changes taking place in the organisation structure require restructuring of the information systems from time to time. In any case, the formal rigour of MIS does not really capture the enormous variety of communication and information flow taking place throughout an organisation, in all its subtleties and styles. It is the effectiveness of the sum total of information flow in the organisation, which can make or break the organisation.

Authority and Accountability

The typical constraint expressed by any manager in an organisation relates to the extent of authority given to him for achieving the objectives for which he is accountable. This constraint may be real or imaginary, significant or insignificant but nevertheless exists in most cases. Partially this arises from the fact that while authority can be and is usually delegated, accountability cannot be delegated. The ultimate accountability for achieving the targeted mission level objectives of the organisation is invariably with the chief executive of the organisation. He may create the whole organisation and assign various functions to divisional heads or departmental heads thus created, along with well defined responsibilities and clearly understood linkages amongst them. However, the mere fact that he has done so, does not imply that he no longer is accountable for the achievements of the organisation as a whole.

Knowing well that the fulfilment of responsibilities requires commensurate availability of resources and discretion of decision making, delegation of authority invariably accompanies assignment of responsibilities. However, in real practice, there may be too little delegation, in case the manager adopts a highly conservative approach. On the other hand, there may be instances when authority has been delegated; however, the organisation culture inhibits sensible exploitation of such delegation. It may also happen that the delegate does not possess the necessary skills to exercise the authority delegated to him.

In many instances, the formal authority does not adequately serve the needs of the functions required to be performed. What is really required in such cases is an informal authority emerging out of the knowledge and skills possessed by the manager. Authority also emerges from the perception of how and to what extent rewards and punishments can be given by a manager to his subordinates. Authority may also emanate from the interpersonal skills of the manager. Thus, it appears that there are two sides to the concept of authority. The formal authority is delegated from the top, the informal authority is taken from below on the strength of one's abilities.

More often than not, in real practice, the authority accountability relationships tend to get blurred. This happens owing to the combined effect of the above factors. A senior manager may actually delegate his accountability to all others and preserve all the authority with himself (and wondering why organisation is not producing results). Another manager may dole out all his authority liberally but fail to define clearly the responsibilities assigned to the subordinates (again finding that something has been achieved by the organisation but wondering whether that was intended to begin with). Most situations would of course fall within such extremes. It is no wonder that typically in organisations, people simply do not know how much authority and responsibility they possess. Organisation charts and job descriptions compound rather than resolve this difficulty.

Authority at times presents itself in ironical forms and deceptive indicators. Very often, authority is not where power is. Consider the designation of the authorised signatory, which represents at best the formal communication of decision. Seldom is an authorised signatory, the actual decision maker. The matter gets to be even more subtle when one is reminded of the fact that even powers are affected by influence. Factors, people and opinions, which influence a decision may originate anywhere, like a breeze wafting to the centre of power, influencing it and passing away. The centre of power absorbs that influence and gets affected and yet it may never show in the organisation structure. It needs a carefully developed sixth sense to know what happened and what can happen to the power of the formal authority position. This organisational reality can almost never be modelled, it can perhaps only be experienced.

Work Design

It is apparent that organisation structures attempt to divide the work required to be performed for meeting organisational objectives into various gradations or positions and thus create work levels. However, it is not uncommon to see gross distortions in work distribution amongst organisational members. There are instances of persons carrying heavy load of work but little authority (though the same is often justified on the ground that work gravitates to the most competent). There are also situations wherein persons have the authority to assign specific tasks to those at the next level but no responsibility for career planning and performance appraisal. In certain other situations, authority for checking and reporting on the work performance of subordinates is given but no authority is given for redirecting or reallocating work. Such distortions, besides being counterproductive with regard to organisational objectives, also act as a source of frustration for various organisational members.

While designing work for various positions, it is important to see that role expectations are clearly defined. These role expectations should take into account organisational objectives and should realistically lay down the responsibilities of each position, commensurate with the organisational objectives. It is also necessary that the linkages of responsibility levels at various positions are clearly brought out so that there are minimal gaps and overlaps. It is also necessary that effective channels of communication and information flow are established up and down and laterlly. At the same time, the work design should aim at reducing rigidity and increasing dynamism and response time of the organisation.

Several types of authority relationships can be provided amongst organisational members. The main line managerial relationship is the most wholesome and comprises assignment of responsibilities, performance appraisal, manpower development, and selection etc. Supervisory relationship is another type in which there is no authority for work allocation and performance appraisal. In the co-ordination type of authority relationship, there is an authority to obtain information on progress but no authority to provide new direction, override disagreements and carry out performance appraisal. In the case of collateral relationship, there is mutual dependence without any authority of one over the other and sustained disagreements can be resolved by reference to some higher authority.

An interesting debate often raised in the context of organisation is whether an organisation structure should be designed in accordance with the quality and competence of existing personnel in the organisation or should this be independent of personalities. Coupled with this is the issue whether work design should correspond to abilities of specific individuals or should this be independent. The answer to these questions is not simple and revolves around yet another debate, that is, whether people exist in the organisation for the sake of the organisation or people (and not so much the organisation) matter. These are in fact extreme views and in real life, either can't he overlooked for the sake of the other.

Thus, while organisation design should be based on objective considerations, a designer has to take cognizance of individual abilities. It is also to be recognised that individual abilities are imbibed through a variety of methods over a period of time. These include formal and informal training, exposure to new responsibility levels and interactions with other functionaries in the organisation. On the other hand, the age factor also has its influence. In the initial stages age usually enhances ability while in the later stage, it may inhibit ability.

Thus, in actual practice, the work allocation to an individual may be such that his ability level is either above, same as, or below the work level actually assigned, resulting in a situation of under-employment, matching employment or overemployment, respectively. In certain instances, the extent of underemployment or overemployment may be serious, virtually jumping to the next lower or higher work level.

It is also not uncommon to see diverse pattern of work allocation, wherein an individual may zoom in and out of successive work level or may find his job extended downward to a lower work level all the time. While these patterns lead to development of interesting case studies for academic community to debate and discuss, they also result in conflicts, turbulations and reduced organisational effectiveness for the organisation where these are observed to be happening.

The basic issues in design of structure then boil down to designing work in terms of responsibility, control and depth, which represent essentially three dimensions of work. In fact, the ultimate organisational intervention is what you can do with work and not people *per se*. There have to be work levels which have to be defined with reference to organisational objectives in mind and with an aim to establish a clear-cut hierarchy of tasks. Obviously these can't be based on perceived mentalities of jobs. It is also to be emphasised that relationship between hierarchy of work level can only be functional. To conclude, one may say that prime design decisions are the following:

(a) Decide basic expected work levels
(b) Decide highest expected work levels
(c) Settle main management levels
(d) Develop divisions/groupings
(e) Deal with any excessive span of control
(f) Determine staff and support roles

Lastly, design is not a one time exercise. It is a continual process. Redesign of organisation structure becomes necessary whenever critical variables or the organisation change. These may include change in technology, change in top management, change in ownership, change in organisation's jurisdiction of functioning etc. Obviously, reorganisation should be carried out as many times as it is warranted as a result of such changes.

A Brief Introduction to the following Case

This chapter dealt with the subject of organisation structures and examined several structural issues faced by an organisation. There was a mention of structureless organisations, signalling the need for new and innovative forms of organisation structures to deal with the enormous environmental complexity facing them.

A matrix organisation is not exactly a new form of organisation structure. It is being increasingly practised in the Indian context by several leading organisations. Most consultancy service organisations are patterned as matrix organisations, as it suits well to the nature of their operations and as it provides them the requisite flexibility to reconfigure based on the emerging needs. Thus, these organisations are able to gear themselves for changing market needs by forming multidisciplinary teams on a project by project basis.

How does a typical matrix organisation operate? How is it able to reconfigure as necessary and respond to the business challenges? What problems does it face? How does it deal with such problems? What lessons can be learnt from a real life example?

The following case deals with matrix organisation in Engineers India Ltd. with a view to highlight some of the above issues. Obviously, the issues have been merely brought out; they need to be further explored by the readers themselves for a better appreciation. It will be a good idea for the student readers to take up this case in a class room/OD laboratory situation.

A Matrix Organisation — The Case of Engineers India Limited*

*This case has been adapted from "Comparative Manpower Planning Practices" by Prof. Vinayshil Gautam (National Publishing House, New Delhi 1988).

1. Background

Engineers India Limited (EIL) was incorporated in 1965 as a joint venture between the Government of India and Bachtel International of the USA. In 1967, through a mutual agreement, EIL became a wholly owned Government enterprise. Today it is one of India's largest and most experienced engineering and consultancy organisations.

Known for its proven ability to solve a variety of engineering problems, EIL applies its extensive specialised knowledge and invaluable experience to the problems of clients both at home and abroad.

The aims and objectives of EIL are as follows:

1. To specialise in the field of process industries, systems design and engineering and project management services;
2. To evaluate, modify and adopt technologies wherever available to suit local requirements;
3. To promote linkages between R&D, process design and equipment manufacturers;
4. To foster and accelerate the development of indigenous technologies including those suitable for application in the rural and small scale sectors;
5. To foster and sustain a strong, highly competitive and dynamic technological workforce;
6. To secure fair monetary returns on its operations both from within and outside the country; and
7. To provide the clients economical services of the highest quality in the field of engineering consultancy and to continue to maintain its preeminence in this field.

EIL's Fields of Operation

Refineries: The concept to commissioning capability of EIL to handle a variety of refinery jobs is geared fully to execute the country's programme aimed at achieving self-sufficiency in petroleum refining by setting up of new refineries, expansion/ revamping of the old one and installation of energy conservation schemes.

Petro-chemicals: EIL has commissioned various plants in India including those of IPCL, BRPL and NOCIL. Turnkey packages are also offered in this field. EIL is actively participating in preparation of technical documents for smooth and efficient technology transfer to the client.

Ocean Engineering: With accumulated experience backed by the in-house R&D, the company is in a position to offer a comprehensive and integrated range of services for a variety of ocean engineering projects. This capability stands out against the backdrop of the nation's commitment to accelerate its onshore and offshore oil production programme.

Metallurgy and Cement: EIL has tremendous capability of carrying out geostatistical studies using computerised techniques.

Aluminium: During the year 1984-85, EIL completed major engineering and procurement activities for Mines, Alumina, and Aluminium project of NALCO.

Paper, Power, Chemicals and Fertiliser: Till now EIL has been able to complete the projects assigned to it by these industries in time.

Pipelines: In addition to the completion of operations on pipelines, vigorous efforts are being made for the identification and approval of a pilot project for transportation of coal slurry through pipelines.

EIL's Services

EIL's extensive portfolio of services include:

1. Feasibility Studies
2. Research and Development
3. Project Management
4. Planning and Scheduling
5. Cost Engineering
6. Process Design
7. Detailed Engineering
8. Procurement
9. Pre-construction Planning
10. Construction Management
11. Commissioning and Plant start up
12. Heat and Mass Transfer Equipment, Design
13. Environmental Engineering
14. Systems Engineering and Electronic Data Processing
15. Specialist Maintenance, Materials Selection and Corrosion Control.

2. Organisation Structure

EIL's treasured assets is its highly professional workforce. Two-third of its entire human resources are engineers, technologists and specialists manning its various departments.

EIL follows the matrix type of organisational structure which is a combination of functional and project forms of organisation. The matrix organisational structure tries to have the advantages of centralisation, for example, economies of scale, risk pooling and specialisation of functional form, and increased co-ordination and motivation of product form of organisational structure.

As the technologies and markets handled by EIL are diverse, task forces of functional centres are formed to solve the problems of a project centre. The members of task forces are selected on the basis of their functional expertise. The leadership of task force is assigned to that functional group that has maximum contribution towards solving the problems for which task force is formed. The task forces are disbanded on completion of the project. This needs a formal structure which retains functional specialisation and related economies of scale. The project centres are the major outputs of the organisation and place demands on the functional centres. The functional centres supply resources to various projects within the organisation. Resources contributed by a functional centre to a project centre are measured in manhours with those of time sheets. The really distinguishing feature of EIL is separation of responsibility of goals of a project from the authority to direct the work necessary which rests with functional manager.

The organisational structure of project management imparts full responsibility to project manager. Functional personnel who perform the work on EIL project have to communicate to their superior, e.g. product service manager will have to communicate with his superior manager of project services. The superiors report to functional heads though project manager assumes full responsibility for performance specification, on a timely basis in accordance with contractual resource limits, he does not have direct authority over functional coordinators. These co-ordinators, however, serve as spokesmen of the project they have been assigned, while reporting to their functional heads.

Project Management

Task Force: In project management, the fields of operations like petro-chemicals, fertilisers and refinery and refinery projects come under the task force system and non-ferrous metallurgy and ocean engineering are set-up as departments which may use either the task force or matrix form of organisation for specific projects. In this set-up, engineering procurement services and Construction Supervision are all brought directly under the project.

The engineering, procurement, and construction departments supply manpower to these task forces and ensure quality of work.

Matrix Structure: In the matrix structure, various parts of the project are executed under the control of relevant functional groups or departments themselves. The work is progressed through project manager.

In practice, most projects are executed by using a combination of two forms. Even task forces get varying functions of work done through central department. The mechanical equipment section under engineering, functions as a central group and not as part of the task force.

A planning and scheduling department which forms part of project services is responsible for detailed scheduling of projects and determined manpower needs at various points of time. Besides, project services include material control and estimating cost control.

The central group of engineering, procurement, and construction provide for manpower to task forces or do project work directly as warranted. Where task forces are involved, the role of central groups with reference to project execution also consists of ensuring uniformity of practice, providing technical guidance and issuing manuals and standards.

The engineering work is done at the headquarters in Delhi. Construction supervision is managed by deputing field officers at various sites. A typed construction organisation has resident construction managers responsible for field engineering, inspection and quality control, site supervision and warehousing besides planning and construction and maintaining accounts for the site. While most procurement work is done from the head office, the department has offices in Bombay and Calcutta mainly engaged in inspection and expediting work in transportation and custom clearances and a London office responsible for overseas purchase.

System and Computer Service Department has its own computer facilities which are used in solving design problems, managing project schedules and also meeting internal data processing and information requirements. The department also undertakes sale of software (particularly for exports) and lets out computer time. The system engineering group undertakes independent business in management studies, O.R., optimization, transportation systems etc.

Situations contingent upon the matrix structure: There are at least three distinct situations which EIL faces due to its matrix structure. These would be dealt with separately:

(a) **Responsibility:** Project managers have ultimate responsibility and functional mangers have technical responsibility for performing work and it is difficult to isolate the responsibility for a given activity when a problem develops. In fact, the responsibility is distributed among the project and functional personnel, thus making the systems of accountability difficult to administer, leading to weak control. There are many potential conflicts, the two most prevalent are conflicts in the resolution of technical problems and in the priorities assigned to various projects by functional groups.

(b) **Insecurity of Project Personnel**: At the completion of a project, the project team is disbanded. So long as the organisation is in growth stage or stable business, they join another project. However, if business is lean or no projects exist, the project personnel may try to artificially increase the duration of project resulting in cost over-runs. In such cases, even functional managers who have permanent organisational units hesitate to come to the rescue of project personnel.

(c) **Difference in World View:** Project manager meets performance, cost and time requirements of projects while functional groups pursue their technical objective without regard to the project goals, in fact functional goals emphasize quality. An effective reward structure is needed to dilute this stress. The reward structure needs to balance the long and short run objectives by rewarding functional group to achieve project targets while maintaining technical competence at the same time. On the other hand, project goals should reflect both the short and long run interests or the organisation wherein long run interest means maintaining good quality of work, thus maintaining client goodwill.

Chapter 5

Nature of Organisational Processes

The Managerial role function over a period of time has grown to be recognised for its characteristic features. From the early perceptions of its being an amorphous combination of skills in planning, work distribution, psychology, sociology, operations research etc., it has now developed an identity of its own. It is all of what is listed above and yet not quite the same, when put together. In many instances, a manager does not have to be so much of an OR expert or a psychologist, as he is expected to have a sound appreciation of the functions that these skills play.

Put simply, a manager has the task of enabling the organisation to perform, to perform effectively, continually and to optimally. To make this possible, the manager has "to put together people variables with organisation or structural variables". The people variables include demographic characteristics, attitudinal aspects, value systems, culture, ethos, work assumptions etc. The structural variables include elements such as task, technology, organisation structure and related factors. Manager's role is to put together these two in a systemic integrated fashion. To do so, he has various instrumentalities at his disposal, such as the ability and prerogative to direct control, recruit, promote reward, punish and train. The list can be considerably expanded.

The above activities are embedded in the processes of communication, co-ordination and control and are integrated by the act of decision making. These organisational processes embrace all gambits of managerial role functions indicated above and are essential for organisational functioning. In fact, these organisational processes provide the necessary integrative mechanisms, thus dovetailing the structural and behavioural dimensions. Thus, it is obvious that inside the seemingly calm exterior of organisations lies a turbulent world. A world full of action, conflicts, accomplishments and failures. A world where decisions are taken all the time by someone in the organisation. A world where communication, whether formal or informal, whether complete or incomplete takes place regularly amongst organisational members. A world where someone needs to co-ordinate and control all that is happening to prevent chaos and to generate action that is in congruity with the organisational objectives. All these are manifestations of organisational processes and the consequences thereof.

Decision Making

Decisions are taken (or made?) by everyone in the organisation. Decision making is in fact an inherent part of work performance by organisational members at various levels. However, the impact of decisions taken at higher levels of management is more profound as compared to those taken at relatively lower levels. A decision taken by an operating level person relating to a specific task being handled by him during the course of his work has implications which are usually confined to similar tasks being performed in the organisation by others. On the other hand, decisions taken at the top management level are bound to have organisation-wide implications. Many decisions may not even be noticed as these are taken almost routinely with predictable outcomes; some others may be landmark decisions may require extensive deliberations and analysis.

As per Simon, decision making requires three distinct and significant phases, namely intelligence, design and choice. Intelligence refers to the activities of understanding the decision scenario, identifying various factors and their interrelationship in the decision scenario, examining the overall environment in which decisions have to be taken and specify criteria for generation of possible alternative decision choices. Design refers to the activity of generating a set of feasible alternatives from which a decision has to be chosen. This requires a creative task of 'constructing' possible courses of action which build a bridge between the desired outcome of a decision and the current situation. The third phase, namely, 'choice' refers to the activity of selecting the most appropriate courses of action, based on an objective assessment of the merits and demerits of various alternatives being considered. This requires explicit or implicit definition of criteria for decision making and analysis of various alternative courses of action in the light of such criteria.

Decisions may be structured, semi-structured or unstructured. Structured decisions are those which have a clear-cut well defined logic. These decisions are usually repetitive, are carried out in most organisations and can be easily programmed, since the procedural steps are clear. In view of their routine and repetitive nature, they are often based on laid down organisational policy and procedures and may be simply ingrained into the 'habit' of the decision makers. The unstructured decisions, on the other extreme, are non-routine, with no clear-cut logic and require creativity for understanding the decision scenario and for generating alternatives. They are therefore not easily programmable, though in the recent years, they can be facilitated with the help of well-designed decision support systems. More often than not, they require a certain degree of insight and intuition in generating alternatives and evaluating them. The semi-structured decisions fall somewhere in the middle. These have no clear-cut logic for generation and evaluation of alternatives. However, these may be amenable to modelling through approximate fitment of the decision scenario to well known management science models.

Irrespective of whether a decision is structured or unstructured or whether it is taken by the top, middle or lower levels of management, information is a key factor which influences the quality of decision making. Availability of requisite information increases the 'determinate' or 'certain' aspects of the possible decisions and thus helps in taking more rational decisions. Information helps in structuring the complexity of the decision scenario and thus facilitates generation of alternatives which can deal with such complexity. Obviously, 'informed' decisions are superior to decisions made in a hurry with little back-up information to enable a true justification of the decision.

Despite all its seemingly objective analysis, decision making tends to be a subjective process. For instance, for most typical decisions, the understanding of the decision scenario is subjective, generation of alternatives largely governed by creative thinking is subjective, determination of evaluation criteria is subjective and actual evaluation of alternatives leading to selection of the most appropriate decision is also subjective. However, the quality of decision making is governed by the maturity and judgemental equilibrium of the decision maker.

Communication

It was mentioned earlier in the book that information is the glue which binds together various components of an organisation. The process through which such a bond takes place is the process of communication.

All organisational actions are preceded by communication amongst organisational members and persons in the outside environment concerned with these actions. Communication is the vehicle through which decisions taken at various levels are transmitted to other levels. Communication is also the vehicle through which the results of actions taken in pursuance of earlier decisions are made known to all concerned. Thus, communication is the lifeline of an organisation and is the reason deterre of all organisational interactions. In fact, the main act of management after decision making is communication.

Communication involves information flow across a structure. It involves transmission of a message by a sender and acknowledgement of the receipt of the message by the receiver. It is therefore asymmetrical, has a specific direction and involves time. Not all communication is verbal. In fact, at times the most persuasive and important part of our communication apparatus is non-verbal—a gesture, accent, manner of speech, posture or even home furnishings and so on.

Communication is successful when it establishes total resonance and fullest understanding amongst the persons communicating with each other. It should be complete in both letter and spirit. However, the whole problem of communication lies in its lack of precision; in distortion of meaning; in superimposition of one's prejudices and complexes in the message being communicated. Thus, not only communication is almost never complete, it can also be counter-productive. In fact, if a person, who is communicating, is misunderstood, he/she is also responsible for the misunderstanding, for having transmitted his/her message at wrong wavelength.

It needs to be emphasised that communication is not merely the flow of information, it is also the flow of attitudes, ideas and opinions. It also involves transmission of feelings and desires. It is a sum of all the acts that a person does when he wants to create understanding in the minds of others. It is a systematic and continuous process of telling, listening and understanding. It provides a basis for common understanding and agreement.

There is just no way an organisation can operate without communication. Communication is the vital link in the chain of events comprising the process of managing a business. It is the single factor which makes organisations viable, effective and enduring communication pervades the entire organisation, connecting and influencing all of its parts.

Most of the manager's work is done by communication, no matter what functional branch he belongs to. A production manager does not run the machinery—he induces others to run it by communicating with them. Selling is almost exclusively communication-based. The sales manager achieves his objectives through communication with his salesmen and salesmen achieve their objectives through communication with customers. Not generally recognised, but true nonetheless is that the prime responsibility of the finance and accounts departments in an organisation is communication of financial information and its implications.

It needs to be emphasized that communication should be oriented to harness organisational objectives. Organisations don't and shouldn't communicate because it is a good thing to do. They should communicate because the success of the organisation depends upon how its objectives are understood and how well that understanding is related to the needs of the market place. Effective communication, therefore, relates directly to the organisation's potential for growth and its need for survival. To be true, growth and survival just don't happen; they need coaxing, cajoling, planning and communication.

An organisation should communicate to promote understanding, productivity, teamwork, and identity. Effectively communicating to each individual his role and his relationship to the roles of others in the organisation enables the individual to work smoothly with his fellow employees.

Communication is also necessary to establish a favourable organisational identity. This means, in general, the overall impression of the organisation in the eyes of its various publics. For employees, customers and stock holders etc., whose exposure to the organisation is both personal and continuous, this identity is built on title more than personalities, products and profits. The desired identity must therefore emerge clearly and consistently from all encounters with the audiences of the organisations.

There are generally four kinds of information communicated to the various audiences of an organisation. These are information on policies, procedures and practices, news of current activities and progress, review of past results and organisational plans and objectives.

All organisations emphasize timeliness in their communications. It is often said that communications should be as instantaneous as possible. However, this statement seems to equate transmission with communications. It assumes that once a message has been put on the line, the message will be received and understood simultaneously by everyone. This assumption does not recognise that obstacles exist in every organisation; obstacles that make the instantaneous flow of communications almost impossible. One of the major obstacles is the structure of the organisation itself. By the time a message has passed through many hands and reached all of its intended receivers, it can't always be timely and accurate. Perhaps, this is the price an organisation has to pay for a structure. There are also circumstantial obstacles such as messages lying for attention with other messages and events; and of course, individual obstacles such as emotion, preoccupation and disinterest.

There is also a relationship between job responsibility and the amount of time and skill devoted to communication activities. As responsibilities increase, more and more time and ability are required for communication. Since, communication plays such a vital role in the organisational and personal success, one would expect that groups and individuals would establish communication goals, set and enforce useful communication policies and carry out procedures to fulfil such goals and policies.

Though conceptually a simple process, communication is perhaps the most difficult part of organisational functioning. More often than not, communication failure (apologetically called "communication gap") is the key reason for dysfunctional conflicts in organisations and many of the typical organisational malaise can be attributed to this.

Effective communication can make a difference between success and failure of an organisation. An organisation person has everything to lose by putting anything less than his best efforts towards effective communication. Since, communication has such a vital influence on the success of an organisation, each individual in the organisation should strive to communicate effectively and to continually improve as a communicator.

Co-ordination

Obviously, the chances of communication failure in organisations are high. This can result in imbalances amongst different constituents of an organisation in terms of various parameters such as resource allocation. Sometimes, these imbalances may result from organisational dynamics involving exercise of power towards furtherance of the interests of one constituent at the cost of others. Such situations dictate the need for an other organisational process, namely co-ordination.

Co-ordination refers to the management of inter-dependencies in work situations. It concerns the interrelationship between tasks which must fit in both form and time into an integrated accomplishment of an overall goal or purpose.

Co-ordination is achieved through exercise of authority available to a person by virtue of his/her hierarchical position in the organisation. It is a metalevel process, implying that this should be the responsibility of a person who is not involved in the carrying out of organisational activities which are being co-ordinated, but who holds a somewhat higher level position in the hierarchy. Co-ordination requires availability of clear-cut criteria for altering the existing balance of resource allocation and is usually facilitated by existence of standard procedures, rules, guidelines and policies. Quite often, analytical methods including management science models provide rational basis for co-ordination decisions. At other times, intuition and gut feeling are important mechanisms for exercising co-ordination effectively. Policy guidelines of course provide a relevant framework within which rational co-ordination decisions can be taken.

Co-ordination is a future oriented process. It involves anticipation of interdependencies and their implications on achievement of organisational objectives as a whole (in contrast to the objectives of the individual departments/units of the organisation). It encompasses minimising sources of conflict by anticipating and avoiding the possibilities of clash of departmental objectives with organisational objectives.

Co-ordination need not necessarily be the role of one single individual at a higher level in the organisation. In many instances, participative decision making is expected to take away significant co-ordination problems since presumably the interests and compulsions of various organisational members would have been taken into account in the process of participative decision making. Besides, participative decision making presupposes mutual trust and collaboration and a common perception of organisation's mission and higher level objectives amongst all participating members.

It may also be seen that co-ordination is more of a facilitating process for achieving a smooth implementation of organisational activities by removing as many impediments as possible. It is triggered by the exercise of control for identifying areas requiring corrective action and by initiating such corrective action.

Control

Control is another very significant organisational process. Very often it is construed to be some kind of a prevention or regulation mechanism. Exercise of control is deemed to imply prohibition of something to someone. However, this is only a distorted version of what control is all about in organisations.

Control refers to the ability of influencing the behaviour of other organisational members in accordance with one's perceived needs of the organisation. Thus, the chief executive of an organisation exercises control over his subordinates by virtue of his ability and discretion to assign roles and allocate resources within the organisation. Exercise of control is thus an inevitable correlate of organisations.

Just as a person at a higher level in the organisation exercises control over persons at lower level, in the same manner, persons at lower level can and do exercise control over persons at higher level. This control may be either explicit (e.g. employee unions posing their demands to the management) or implicit (an employee expects higher rewards and gets them because he performed in accordance with the expectations from his senior in the organisation). Thus, the total amount of control in the organisation can be seen as a function of the amount of exchange involving compliance. In fact, the total amount of control in an organisation, should be considered as an index of the degree of systems proneness organisation.

It may also be mentioned that planning and control are two sides of the same coin. Planning involves laying down targets of performance; control requires taking corrective action to ensure that the actual performance is in tune with the targets of performance and in revising performance targets and thereby initiating another iterative planning function. Thus, planning and control are symbiotic; one can't exist without the other.

Control smacks of autocratic management and interference. This is because, more often than not, in practice, the persons exercising control transgress the boundaries of control. No longer do they restrict their own role in monitoring performance against standards and initiate policy changes for corrective action, but they tend to get more and more involved in the day-to-day execution of tasks which they are meant to control. Thus, control degenerates into undue interference. Very often, this is resorted to when these tasks symbolize something prestigious or financially attractive.

Information is a key parameter for exercising control. A typical control situation involves a feedback loop wherein the actual outcome of certain organisational actions is compared with the desired outcome and the resultant gap is used to trigger changes in the organisational actions. Similarly, the feed forward mode of control involves changing the organisations' plans of action based on the gap between anticipated and desired outcomes of organisational actions. Both these modes of control require information on the results of typical organisational actions, in terms of actual or likely degree of goal achievement.

Communication, co-ordination and control are three important organisational processes which make an organisation dynamic and vibrant. If these processes are carried out smoothly, the organisation will be an effective one; if, however, there are certain impediments to the smooth functioning of these processes, some degeneration in organisational performance is expected to occur. A possible source of such degeneration could be the interplay of behavioural factors. These will be examined in the next chapter.

A Brief Introduction to the Following Case

This chapter has dealt with organisational processes and their importance for the effective functioning of an organisation. It has dealt in length with decision making, communication, co-ordination and control. It has emphasized several underlying concepts behind these managerial role functions and also established a linkage between them.

The Case of International Airport Authority of India, that follows, demonstrates how in a real life situation, the organisational processes are instrumental in almost achieving a turn-around for an organisation known to be slow in responding to its own performance targets. Witness the changes brought about by the chief executive in the processes of decision making, communicating the decisions, co-ordinating all the activities and controlling the progress.

Of course, the case is not merely concerned with effectiveness of organisational processes. It is as well concerned with the quality of leadership and with the need for innovation and creativity in carrying out even the seemingly routine functions. It is also concerned with creating a new organisation culture. But then, in an organisational setting in the real life, can one really look at the organisational processes separated from other factors?

Like in every real life situation, there is a time dimension attached to the present case. The organisation will obviously change over time; however, the issues underlying this case will not change very drastically. On the other hand, there will be an enlarged framework for discussion and exploration in an academic forum. The student readers are advised to take it up as a laboratory exercise in OD.

International Airport Authority of India — A Case of Effective Organisational Processes

The commissioning of the second terminal of the Indira Gandhi International Airport is a good example of how dynamic leadership can be used to manage organisations better. The airport was targeted to be commissioned in May 1986; however, as late as March 1986, it appeared as if the organisation was without any direction or vision. There had been no chief executive in position for quite some time, the staff was demoralised and the officers 'disoriented'. The 'new' incumbent, Mr. N.K. Singh, made an assessment that nearly six months will be required to commission the airport properly as against only one and a half months available. There were two choices, one to reschedule the date of commissioning and the second, to somehow ensure that the target date was adhered to. Despite clear-cut difficulties, the second choice was adopted by Mr. Singh primarily with a view to re-build the credibility of the organisation and thereon build upon the morale of the people in the organisation.

Once the choice was made, the leadership qualities of Mr. Singh were virtually put on the test. Several creative and innovative approaches were made use of by him in steering the organisation towards achieving its targets. For instance, he introduced a system of periodic monitoring and controlling the work progress, thereby ensuring that everyone concerned with the construction project carried out the tasks in the given time schedule. Wherever the situation warranted taking corrective actions, and collective actions, decisions were taken on the spot through collective discussions. In the whole process, it was ensured that a pace was set up and maintained by the top leadership. This was coupled with building up of a sense of enthusiasm amongst the officers and staff. It was experienced that once the group of people is sufficiently enthused, they were willing to put in for more than normal working hours and achieve even the very difficult targets.

Apart from the above, there were several other innovative practices adopted by the top management. For instance, it took upon itself the task of developing and training contract employees, a task which is invariably considered out of purview of an organisation. However, it was felt that unless these employees, who had to make substantial contributions to the needs of the organisation, were tuned to its ethos and expectation, they will not give their best.

Another significant initiative taken by the Management was the setting up of Institute of Airport Management. It was developed into a networking organisational model. Core faculty were made use of by the institute for key areas and these were supplemented through galaxy of resources available outside. The institute took upon itself the responsibilities of training not only the executives of IAAI, but also those of other related organisations working together under the roof of the airport, namely customs, security, airlines etc.

IAAI is a unique organisation in the sense that it has to co-ordinate the functioning of as many as 36 organisations operating under a single roof. It was indeed a challenge for the organisation to make all the concerned organisations and persons become aware of their interdependence and be responsive to the areas of operations of the others. Another significant step taken was to introduce a virtually on-line MIS, which would provide the information on all key issues of airport operations to the top management. This kind of MIS was helpful to ensure that all the agencies worked in greater co-ordination with each other, or that there were no undue delays in matters such as baggage handling. The challenge of fine tuning the integration of various functions performed by different agencies/organisations, at the airport was thus strived to be met.

In a separate interview, the first chief executive of the IAAI commented that there is always a need to push and dislocate something, to bring in something new, and desirable. He felt that people invariably respond to feedback, which ought to be given in ample measures. He also expressed the sentiment that a transition has to take place from sympathy to empathy if the feedback has to be effectively utilised for organisational purposes.

Chapter 6

The Behavioural Dimension

Issues related to organisational structures and processes have been covered in this book till the end of previous chapter. However, the study of organisations is far from complete without discussing the behavioural dimension. Human beings are the most important constituent of organisations and the complexities of human behaviour add their own turns and twists to organisational performance. If harnessed effectively, human behaviour can add synergy to its otherwise well designed structure, procedures, rules and regulations. However, if the human behaviour for whatever reason, manifests itself in actions and postures damaging to the organisation, one is bound to witness the decay of organisation sooner or later. Irrespective of the nature of technology inducted, an organisation, in the final analysis it is the organisational personnel who are the prime movers of the technology in the organisation. Despite the high degree of sophistication of technology, people can't be wished away from an organisation. Organisations in fact not only have to deal with the organisational personnel, but also have to make an effective use of their energies, skills, creativity and group dynamics for meeting organisational objectives.

However, it is easier said than done. Human behaviour is governed by a variety of internal and external factors. Motivation of organisational personnel results from inherent human characteristics as well as organisation dependent situations. The fact that organisational personnel do not work in isolation but in groups, brings in the issues of interpersonal relationships and group behaviour. Leadership provided by managers at various levels influences interpersonal relationships, group behaviour and individual motivation. Leadership itself may be provided in varying styles and with differing emphasis on tasks and relationships and yet with similar results. With all their permutations and combinations, the behavioural issues dominate the scenario of organisational functioning.

This chapter discusses in detail the behavioural dimension of organisations and gives a brief overview of motivation, interpersonal and group dynamics, leadership and other related issues.

Understanding Human Behaviour

Perhaps, the most fundamental question in a social context, having a bearing in the organisational context, is that of understanding human behaviour. The typical issues are: why do persons behave as they behave and how their behaviour can be modified? At the social level, two extreme views have been expressed about the basic human traits. One view, that of Hubbs, is that life in the history and state of nature was nasty and brutish. The civil society came into existence primarily to protect the weak against the strong. The second view, that of Locke, which is diametrically opposite, is that life in the history and state of nature was idyllic and blissful. The civil society came into existence, primarily to preserve these qualities of life. Which one of the above views is true, is extremely difficult to state. Perhaps, there are shades of truth in both of them. As per Schopinhaur, human being has two basic desires—self-love and self-hate. All human actions are governed by this duality.

Another view on human behaviour, put in simple words, is that human behaviour is controlled by the perceived consequences of human behaviour. These perceived consequences may result from past memories of rewards and punishments associated with the behaviour or may occur from projections/correlations of new and uncertain situations with prior experiences, which may have been good or bad. It also needs to be stated that human behaviour is contingent upon the situation. Not only that, in apparently similar situations, the human behaviour may be manifested in highly divergent ways.

One can conclude from the above that human nature is not only complex, but also highly variable. Also, monocausal interpretation of human nature can be totally misleading.

Motivation

Irrespective of the difficulties in understanding human nature, human beings have to be managed in organisations. One important aspect of managing human beings is to motivate them. This essentially implies developing conditions in the organisation which make the employees committed and involved in achieving organisational objectives. This is a key managerial function regardless of the size of the organisation or the activities it is engaged in. In fact, motivation of subordinates to achieve organisational objectives is a continual management responsibility.

The word motivation has evolved from 'motive', which means 'an inner state that energises, activates or moves'. Thus, motivation essentially means creating an inner urge to perform. Employee motivation to work towards meeting organisational objectives depends upon their perceived degree of need satisfaction from such working. However, motivation can't be directly observed and measured.

There is no rational explanation for motivation as yet. Views on causes of motivation include sociological, biological and psycho-analytical. As per the sociological view, people, events, values and customs determine the action of people in a society. As per the biological view, physical and biological forces cause specific behaviour patterns. The psycho-analytical view attributes motivation to unconscious feelings and sentiments.

One debatable hypothesis is that fear is the biggest motivator. This hypothesis may be true provided the word 'fear' is used in the widest possible context. Fear may include the fear of punishment and also the fear of loss of reward. Or, it may be the fear of the unknown!

It needs to be emphasised that there are limits to motivation. Through motivation, one can't give what is not there. It is important to realise these limits because it accentuates the significance of selection and recruitment procedures. Motivation brings out a potential or curbs an aberration, however it does not create abilities and performance *ab initio*. Fortunately, for persons and organisations, there is always a large reservoir of human potential to be tapped.

What the western theorists on motivation can't be expected to appreciate because of the limits of the universe of their study is the fact that in certain cultures, one is motivated perhaps in a most deterministic fashion by the urge to gain acceptance in the group with which he emotionally identifies. McGregor, Hertzberg or even Maslow never entered the debate of how in various cultures, ascribed status remains superior to achieved status and indeed how achieved status is, ultimately, the route to the ascribed status. Nevertheless, it is useful to look at what these management theorists have to say about motivation.

Motivation and Human Behaviour

All theories of motivation are grounded in the basic assumptions about human nature and behaviour. Two extreme viewpoints, having a strong resemblance and perhaps originating from the extreme views of Hobbs and Locks about the emergence of civil society, are referred to in the organisation literature, describing certain basic human traits. These are brought out clearly in McGregor Theory X and Theory Y. Theory X describes a set of assumptions about human behaviour which have a rather negative tone. These are as follows:

1. The average human being has an inherent disliking for work and will avoid it if he can.
2. Because of this human characteristic of disliking work, most people must be coerced, controlled, directed or threatened with, punishment to get them to put forth adequate effort towards the achievement of organisational objectives.
3. The average human being prefers to be directed, wishes to avoid responsibility, has relatively, little ambition and wants security above all.

The opposite view on human nature contained in McGregor's Theory Y is reflected in the following statements:

1. The expenditure of physical and mental effort in work is as natural as play or rest.
2. Man will exercise self-discretion and self-control in the service of objectives to which he is committed.
3. Commitment to objectives is a function of the rewards associated with their achievement. The most significant of such rewards, e.g. the satisfaction of ego and self-actualisation needs, can be direct products to effort directed towards organisational objectives.
4. The average human being, under proper conditions, learns not only to accept but to seek responsibility.
5. The capacity to exercise a relatively high degree of imagination, ingenuity and creativity in the solution of organisational problems is widely, not narrowly, distributed in the population.

Maslow's Hierarchy of Needs

An interesting theory of motivation is provided by Maslow through his conceptualisation of hierarchy of needs. As per this theory, human needs can be grouped into five categories. These are physiological, safety, social, esteem and self-actualisation needs. Initially, human beings are concerned with satisfying their basic physiological needs such as food, shelter etc. Once they are satisfied on this front, their next priority is to satisfy their safety needs. The social needs come next and if satisfied, the esteem needs become predominant. Last, but not the least are the self-actualisation needs which achieve importance for the individuals who have been satisfied in terms of their physiological, safety, social and esteem needs. Thus, there exists a hierarchy of needs, the satisfaction of which becomes the motivating factor.

It will be useful to illustrate and explain the meaning of various types of needs. Physiological needs as mentioned above include food, clothing and shelter and are the first and foremost requirements of an individual. Until they are satisfied, it is unlikely that the human behaviour will be motivated by any other factor. However, it does not mean that this satisfaction has to be absolute. After a reasonable level of satisfaction has been attained on this front, the motivation of satisfying the safety/security needs will become dominant. These include concern for physical safety and for being able to continually provide for satisfaction of physiological needs in the future. The security needs may be manifested at a personal level or in a work situation. For instance, one typical security need may pertain to job security.

The social needs pertain to the urge to form part of a group or groups. The human being wants to have associations with others; he wants to belong to others and be accepted by others. He seeks to form alliances and relationships with others. Obviously, this need is manifested only after the physiological and security needs have been met with.

The next level of hierarchy is the esteem needs. Individuals seek prestige and status. They continually evaluate themselves *vis-à-vis* others and may conclude that they deserve respect from others in view of their achievements in life. Their own self-esteem is built up, sometimes to the extent of large inflated egos. They need a continual satisfaction of their ego by being praised by others. Many actions carried out by individuals who have achieved moderate to high satisfaction of their physiological, security and social needs are aimed at satisfying their esteem needs. And yet, these needs are difficult to satisfy because one's self-esteem is likely to greatly differ with the perceptions of others.

The self-actualisation needs come in the end. These are the most sublime form of human needs and are aimed at excellence, perfection, professional achievement and the like. The individual at the self-actualisation level has presumably satisfied all the other level of needs to a reasonable extent and is therefore looking forward to achieve his potential in one or more fields of life. All actions on his part are directed towards meeting this kind of needs.

It may be mentioned that the manifestation of various types of needs does not take place at the exclusion of all others. At no time, all types of needs can be fully satisfied, and all needs are operational to some extent. However, the model seems to be applicable in a general sense, in that there is typically a predominance of one type of needs for an individual at a given state of his work life.

Herzberg's Motivation Maintenance Theory

Herzberg's motivation maintenance theory provides another framework for studying motivational aspects of human behaviour. This is also referred to as the two factor theory of motivation because it describes two independent sets of factors, not opposite to each other, which are related to motivation. These two sets of factors are called maintenance factors and motivation factors. Maintenance factors are those that make people unhappy or dissatisfied with the jobs. Motivation factors are those that make people happy or satisfied. It has been observed that when maintenance factors are not present on the job, the result is dissatisfied employees. If motivational factors are also found, they produce high level of job satisfaction and motivation; but if they are not present, they do not produce dissatisfaction.

Some of the maintenance factors include interpersonal relations, company policy, working conditions, supervision, job security etc. These factors, by and large, correspond to the social, safety and physiological needs in the Maslow's hierarchy of needs. The motivational factors, on the other hand, include achievement, recognition, work itself, responsibility and advancement.

It may be worthwhile to illustrate and further elaborate the maintenance and motivation factors and their implications. It was hypothesised by Herzberg that when people felt dissatisfied with their jobs, they were concerned with the conditions that surrounded the jobs themselves. These maintenance factors involved the environment and conditions in which work was accomplished. Maintenance factors include physical working conditions, job security, company policies and administration, social and interpersonal relations and pay and economic benefits. If any of these factors is not present to the liking of the employees, the result is dissatisfaction. Providing the maintenance factors does not result in enhanced employees output capacity, but prevents losses done to workers restricting performance.

M. Scott Myers summarised the effect of maintenance factors by stating that these factors are characterised by the fact that they inspire little positive sentiments when provided, but incite strong negative reactions when removed.

Satisfying factors that involve feeling of achievement, professional growth and recognition are referred to as motivators. These factors are capable of having a positive effect on job satisfaction, often resulting in an increase in one's total output capacity.

Interpersonal and Group Dynamics

An interesting observation in the context of the organisations is that the human behaviour is significantly influenced by the interpersonal associations and formation of groups. These associations are caused by formal authority relationships; however, they are invariably informal in nature.

The formation of groups takes place when people are thrown together on account of work allocations. Typically, if employees are located together at the same place, they are likely to come close to each other and observe each other's values, beliefs and interests. When two or more people start sharing each other's values and interests, they tend to form a group. Soon, the group starts developing an emotional bond, starts prescribing its own norms and objectives and therefore, becomes almost an organisation in itself.

The perceptions, beliefs and attitudes of individuals are strongly influenced by the groups of which they are members. The groups dictate their own values and all members of the group are expected to conform to these values. The price of group membership then becomes the approval of group values and willingness to conform to them.

Besides group values, one witnesses the emergence of group norms. Of course, it can be stated that the group values dictate the group norms. Many times, these norms may relate to output levels which should be attained by individual members of the group. Members exceeding the norms may face censure from other group members. Deviants are either made to conform through the application of group morality or are forced to exit the group. Sometimes, the groups may split when a sizeable number of group members choose to stick together and separate out from the parent group based on their own distinct group values and norms.

It may be relevant to cite here some research findings of Cartwright and Zander at the Research Centre for Group Dynamics. As per these authors, groups either aim to achieve specific groups goals or aim to maintain or strengthen the group itself. The group leaders endeavour to achieve both these objectives concurrently.

One significant consequence of group dynamics is that motivation of individuals is dictated by group values and norms. For instance, the Hawthrone Experiments conclusively established the fact that the groups control the output of workers, more than anything else. Another consequence of group dynamics is the natural tendency for existence of group conflicts. Up to a point, the conflict amongst groups is manageable, perhaps even desirable. The sense of competition amongst groups helps in bringing out the best and the most creative elements of all organisational members. However, beyond that, the intergroup conflicts can be counter-productive. Very often, confrontation postures are taken by the groups, suboptimal actions are encouraged and the activities of competitive actions are encouraged and the activities of the competitive group sabotaged so that the opposite groups is brought down in terms of its acceptability in the organisations.

Interpersonal and group dynamics can often tend to be so complex that organisations may get lost into their trap and cease to be effective. More often than not, the consequences of group dynamics are negative and not nourishing for organisational health. The top managements of the organisation have to assume a conscious role in managing group dynamics and minimise its adverse implications. They have to seek and maintain an acceptable level of group conflict which if handled properly, can enhance the achievement of organisational objectives.

Leadership

It is apparent that for managing group dynamics and for motivating the employees, the manager should be capable of influencing the subordinates to alter their behaviour. These qualities are called the qualities of leadership.

A leader is one who influences others to achieve an objective in a given situation. Obviously, as per this definition of leadership, it is not essential that the leader should be at a superior position in the organisation.

What is important is that through his thoughts and actions, the leader should be able to make others, irrespective of their levels and positions, act and behave in accordance with the most important objectives as perceived by the leader. This ability may be derived by virtue of the formal authority which the leader may enjoy or it may be informal authority, earned by the leader's better social acceptability, knowledge and competence or any other factors/traits. It is apparent that a leader does not have to be a manager, however, a manager should also be a leader.

"Leadership is an illusive art, practised more on the basis of feel than on the basis of cognitive knowledge". Several studies have been undertaken by various researchers to study how leadership emerges. Many research works have attempted to identify leadership traits commonly shared by leaders, but it has not been possible to isolate a few common leadership traits. More often than not, one needs to have an intuitive sensing of leadership. However, it may be worthwhile mentioning a few leadership traits believed to be applicable in many situations. These include awareness of group attitudes by the leader, ability of the leader to carry out abstract thinking, emotional stability of the leader and closeness of the self-perception of the leader to that of his group. It also needs to be mentioned that leadership is not merely a function of the leadership traits, but is also dependent upon the perceptions of the followers of the leader. It is observed that the followers typically follow those leaders who in their view best help them satisfy their (i.e. follower's) needs. It is therefore necessary that the leader must be aware of the needs, norms and behaviour patterns of the persons whom he expects to lead.

Schools of Leadership

There are two basic and often opposing schools of thought about the origin and development of leadership. These are the 'Actor School' and the 'Born Leader School'. Advocates of the actor school assume that managers are like active players in a drama, relatively flexible and capable of altering their behavioural patterns even in the last years of life. They are apt at exercising conscious and rational control over their own behaviour. They adapt continuously to new rules and demands posed on them by their organisations. They emphasize the use of management education to convert executives to a participative style. In accordance with the assumptions of this school, many executives have been exposed to programmes, stressing humane and productive aspects of participative leadership. These programmes have varied in their brand, with their focus ranging from/to team decision making, joint goal setting and listening skills.

Advocates of the born leader school assume that a leader's style is deeply routed in his personality, which is a complex product of genetic inheritance and maturation process. As per this school, each manager's style is highly individual acquired over many years after an unconscious pattern arising out of gained values, attitudes and beliefs. However, it is contended under this school that managers can't easily adapt to new patterns of behaviour, as they become older.

Thus, to compare the two schools of leadership, it can be said that as per actor school, leadership behaviour can be taught while as per the born leader school, leadership behaviour is individually developed. Further, as per actor school, the leadership behaviour is largely determined by external cues from the environment while as per the born leader school, leadership behaviour is largely determined by internal personality characteristics.

Leadership Styles

In the management literature, three leadership styles have been identified. These are autocratic or authoritarian, democratic or consultative and free rein or *laissez faire*. The autocratic or authoritarian style is characterised by formal authority, rewards and punishments. In this kind of leadership all decisions are taken by the leader and the followers are expected to carry out the tasks assigned to them as per such decisions. The acceptability of such decisions by the followers depends upon their perception of the strength of the formal authority enjoyed by the leader. However, in its absolute form, this style of leadership is fairly uncommon, since in the present day work environment, it is difficult to conceive of persons who will meekly accept an autocratic leader and abdicate their rights in arriving at decisions in which they have a stake.

The democratic or consultative style is characterised by sharing of ideas with followers while taking decisions. This sharing may range from one extreme, wherein the followers express their opinions but leave the final decisions to be taken by the leaders, to the other extreme, wherein the followers not only express their opinions, and ideas, but also take decisions collectively. This style appears to be the most acceptable in current work environment, since it is in tune with the social environment of democracy.

The third style of leadership, namely free rein or *laissez faire* style is characterised by a minimal leadership role played by the leader. At best, the leader provides information, material and facilitation for decision making. The followers (it may not be even appropriate to call them followers) arrive at decisions on their own and it often appears that the leader has abdicated the leadership role. The consequence, of course, can be that the decisions taken may be suboptimal and counter-productive in the context of organisation as a whole.

Participative Leadership

As commonly understood, participative leadership involves one's subordinates in the decision making process, maintaining free flowing and honest communication, remaining easily accessible, stressing development of subordinates, expressing consideration and support for subordinates and having willingness to change. Thus, a participative leader is a sensitive, extrovert, emotive person, who actively stays in close contact with his subordinates, is attuned to their needs and is interested in their training and development.

A participative leader keeps subordinates aware of high performance expectations, even if this means any directive action within an overall participative style. He is more concerned with the psyche of his subordinates rather than the fruits of their labour.

There is considerable divergence of opinion amongst management educators and organisation theorists on what is meant by participative leadership. It is taken to mean differently as 'group decision making, mutual goal setting and listening more and talking less'. However, there is very little understanding about how the participation message is absorbed at the managerial level and what concrete behavioural characteristics managers actually associate with participation. It is also not very clear whether managers differ widely in their specific interpretation of participative leadership or if there is a really uniform understanding. Further, even if managers understand or agree in practical aspects of participative leadership, it is not clear whether they believe that participation will lead to more effective results.

There appears to be a loose link between perceptions of effectiveness and participative leadership. A manager guided exclusively by effectiveness criteria will favour actions that are not included in a strict interpretation of participative leadership. Lastly, the yardsticks for measuring accomplishments of participative leadership are not reliable.

If the idea of participative leadership is taken seriously, the leaders are going to be bombarded with questions whether the established methods are best. In fact managers at all levels will have to discover new ways to assert leadership.

Managerial Grid

It is obvious that a manager should first and foremost be acceptable to his subordinates as a leader. He has to adapt his style of leadership to ensure that he can in some way or the other help the subordinates to satisfy their needs. This requires in turn, that he establishes fairly strong concern for personal relationships. However, swinging of the pendulum to the other extreme of maintaining personal relationships at the cost of accomplishment of organisational tasks has its own perils. No sooner the manager may find himself replaced because he is not in a position to achieve organisational objectives for which he was assigned the role of a manager in the first place.

On the other hand, a manager may have a very high concern for task accomplishment. He may consider maintenance of personal relationships and the corresponding concern for persons, only as a means to an end and not an end in itself. So far so good; unless of course a manger gets unduly obsessed with the concern for task accomplishment at the cost of concern for personal relationships. If a manger takes such an extreme posture, he may ultimately deprive himself of the acceptability by his subordinates and thus, may cease to be a leader.

It is apparent that a harmonious balance has to be maintained between the concern for task accomplishment and the concern for people. This idea has been presented in the form of what is termed as 'Managerial Grid', by Blake and Mouton. In this Grid, five leadership styles have been identified as listed below:

(a) *Country Club*

This style is characterised by highest concern for people and not much concern for task accomplishment. This style may lead to popularity but may rank very low on effectiveness.

(b) *Impoverished*

In this style, the leader exercises very small concern for task accomplishment as well as for people. No wonder, in this kind of style, leader is virtually non-existent and whatever is achieved by the organisation is achieved despite the leader and not because of the leader.

(c) *Task*

This style is characterised by the highest concern for task accomplishment and not much concern for people. It is a difficult style and can be successful only if the task organisation is such that human elements have a minimal role in task accomplishment. However, this style is risky and sooner or later, the subordinates may get alienated from the manager.

(d) *Team*

This style is perhaps the ideal style, though not easy to acquire. This involves a high concern for tasks as well as people simultaneously. If achieved and pursued successfully, this style can provide dovetailing of the organisational and individual objectives and consequently synergy of efforts to the satisfaction of both.

(e) *Middle of the Road*

This is the balanced style, modulated by the realisation that the idealistic team style may not be easily attainable. It is therefore desirable that a fair balance is attained in task accomplishment as well as concern for people, without undermining one to achieve gains in another. This perhaps is the most realistic leadership style.

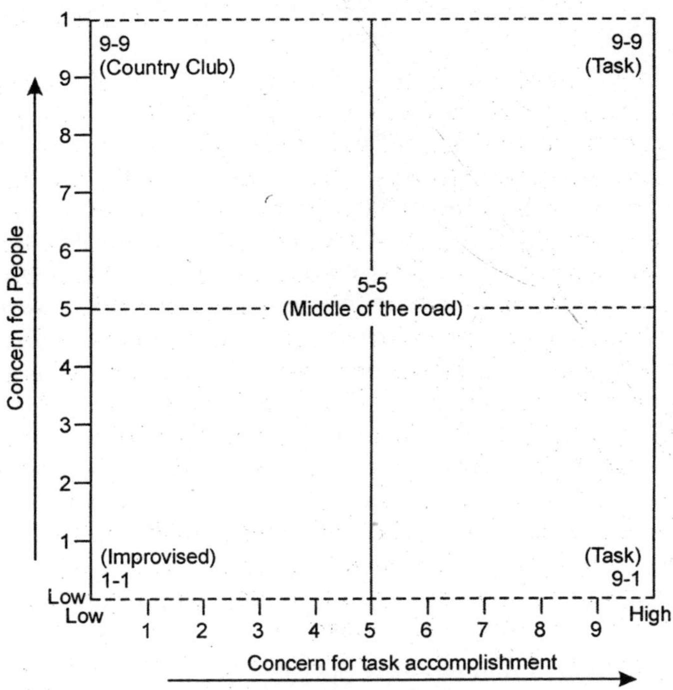

Figure 6.1: Illustration of leadership styles schematically.

Concluding Comments

It will be wrong to assume that the behavioural dimension has been completely travested in the preceding pages. In fact, the ocean of behavioural patterns witnessed in organisations can never be fathomed. A limited analysis based on research studies and empirical observations is like taking a sample of ocean water, analysing it and attributing its properties to the entire ocean. All we can say about the behavioural dimension is that it is like a pandora box which has to be opened if an organisation has to function. However, it should be handled carefully because sensitivities of a very high order are involved. The organisation members themselves need ways and means to deal with the behavioural dimension in the organisation, to be able to achieve their own personal objectives from the organisation.

This points towards the needs for developing and adopting coping strategies, both for the organisation as well as for the individual. These aspects have been dealt with in the subsequent two chapters.

A Brief Overview of the Following Interview

It is rare to be face to face with authors, whose writings you admire. If and when such an opportunity comes, what will you do? Obviously, apart from admiring them, you will like to interact with them to obtain greater insights into what they have been expressing through their writings. You will like to hear from them their own personal findings about the practicability of the concepts propounded by them.

The 'managerial grid' is one such concept, which has been just covered in this chapter. It is, therefore, appropriate that when the authors of managerial grid are face to face with us, we make use the opportunity to conduct an interview with them. The following interview with Dr. Robert Blake and Dr. Jane Mouton is an attempt to seek an elaboration on the concept of managerial grid.

Needless to reiterate that the subjects for discussion in OD are never segregated in a neat and clean manner. Thus, it is only to be expected that a discussion on managerial grid will not be confined only to the managerial grid, but will also transcend to other vital organisational issues such as the national environment and the organisation culture.

How about carrying on the discussion further in your OD laboratory or in your office setting, as appropriate?

More on the Managerial Grid: An Interview with Dr. Robert Blake and Dr. Jane Mouton

Dr. Vinayshil Gautam in conversation with Dr. Robert Blake and Dr. Jane Mouton best known for their concept of managerial grid had to document the following:

Question: We are of course very delighted to have both of you Dr. Blake and Dr. Mouton, with us and as you are yourself aware that your work on the Managerial Grid has made a seminal contribution to the design of management systems and world organisations. I was hoping to use this opportunity to elicit from you your perceptions on how this concept is currently being used in some of the organisations to develop more effective work situation. You may wish to choose your own illustrations that would help us in applying some of these concepts in our own environment.

Dr. Blake: Well, we are delighted to be here. Only this morning we had a chance to skip for a moment away from the conference and go to the University of Delhi to meet a group of Faculty and students, which was very stimulating to us. We gave an example here in the conference and I will just repeat that first. It involved the effectiveness with which the people in the cock-pit, flying officers in the cock-pit integrate their resources in order to do a better job of accident prevention. The evidence that brought this project into being was that 80 per cent of modern jet liners and cock-pit aviation aircraft, 80 per cent of those accidents are not accountable by air to ground communications or equipment failure, or insufficient time or technical crew competence or weather. Twenty per cent are explained by those factors, 80 per cent are not. Just to come to the other end of the story, it was concluded from a series of experiments that the real problem was one of leadership in the following way: That when a crisis loomed, the Captain mobilises authority in himself and commands the other members to take specific actions.

Dr. Mouton: This is what common sense says should happen in a crisis—one person should take over centralised control of the Group. Now this is a very responsible behaviour, but one that other hand in doing so the Captain shuts out the inputs from the First officer and the Second officer. So, one-third of the brains of the crew are being used to solve very complex problems. In these accidents, there is sufficient time to get input from the others and to test the soundness of the Captain thinking against the soundness of recommendations made by others. So, here is a case where the interaction of the crew, the teamwork among the crew is the explanation of those 80 per cent of accidents, all of which were adjudged to be avoidable. Now, that is an important critical significant factor of leadership and the conclusion from the Grid point of view is that the 9-1 behaviours of taking strong control and commanding a reaction without finding an input is very destructive, very potentially risky. The option is a 9-9 approach which mobilises as much resource as possible. So this is one example.

Question: Since, we all recognise that there are cultural factors which come into organisations with people as part of their cultural baggage as it were, it would be obviously one of the objectives of training inputs in conditioning these people to certain organisational ways of functioning: because people have different perception of self images and they have to be brought within manageable limits within the objectives of the organisation to make it a performing organisation. And that is where, I think, your concept of Managerial Grid becomes really effective. What would be some of your suggestions in the way of the design of these training programmes to bring about these commonly shared uniform perceptions amongst the people who have newly joined an organisation to make them a part of the team, to make it possible for us to implement the Managerial Grid perceptive?

Dr. Mouton: First of all a very important part when we think of training programme which deals with behaviours is that the methodology used should be self-convincing. A person is unlikely to change if someone says do it this way, particularly if they say it in a coercive way. So, this means that it is very important for people to have situations where they can compare the effectiveness of different styles of leadership and then draw their own conclusions as to what is more and less effective. This is particularly important in the area of teamwork, because some styles of leadership are very ineffective, the teams having other styles are much more effective. Also, a person needs to know his or her own leadership style and we know and I am sure everyone else has had the same experience. We asked someone what his leadership style was like, he feels he is doing a good job and he is very likely to say on the grid that he is 9-9, because his intentions are good and that is what he would like to see himself doing. However, if a colleague in a learning setting looks at the same behaviours, he is able to give the person more objective feedback as to what in fact he is doing. This is a source of self-correction for an individual to help him to learn to change.

Dr. Blake: I can give another case study which is somewhat closer to Asian circumstances. This involves the Donald Douglas Company, the aircraft manufacturer. They produce the DC-3, the DC-7 and the DC-10 and so on and so forth. The Donald Douglas signed a technology transfer contract with the Government of China. The idea was that in 10 years the Donald Douglas, working with the Chinese Government would engage in helping the Chinese manufacturing function or activity, to be competent in aircraft manufacture. Now, the Americans came to Shanghai. They joined forces with the Shanghai Aircraft Organisation and immediately started training—the Grid type training. But, they had terrible culture conflicts. One conflict that rose very quickly was that the Americans were disregarding the living habits of the Chinese and demanding people to work on a schedule for which the transport system of China was inappropriate. People could not get to work in spite of the fact that they were required to be there at certain fixed scheduled times. That was one problem. Another was that the Chinese felt very much pushed by free enterprise logic, that had concern for the Dollar, but had far less appropriate degree of concern for people as human beings. So, after they had been in the grid, top people, they stepped away from the work and spent several days designing what would be ideal as the basis for co-operation between the Americans and the Chinese and they reached to very relevant conclusions: that the Americans should keep themselves focused on operations and being effective.

By the same token the Chinese should not man the factory based on Communist party loyalty. They should man the factories based upon the competence to receive technology transfer. And I can go through a number of other changes, but here is whether a cultural baggage from one culture was right in a deep friction with the cultural values from another culture and the only way, therefore, at least the way they used to escape from cultural conflicts and negative history, was to come to a shared agreement and how would be the sound values for that top group of Chinese-Americans managers to co-operate. Since that time, the tensions have vastly reduced. This is the case of building a team, not trying to go around the problem but to confront the problems and by identifying them, learn how to put them aside in order in work.

Question: Therefore, obviously the recipe would have to be situation specific, in the larger embedding of the principles of management.

Dr Blake: Always culture specific. The way the Grid works is that we will say and this does not have to be accepted because it is a debatable point, but we would say that our research from all-over the world tells us that the grid is a very comprehensive way that people think regardless of whether they are Chinese or Japanese or Americans or Indians or Afghans. Now, Americans and Afghans do not think the same way. An Afghan comes out on the grid in quite a different grid style than an American, but the systems bring out the cultural similarities and differences and so you don't have to change the learning system to fit in the culture. But, you have to study the specific culture to get the main advantage from the grid system.

Chapter 7

Coping Strategies: Individual

One thing unique about organisations is that they have no existence without organisational members. They can cope with their environment only to the extent the organisational members provide them these capabilities. The organisational members themselves require a constant nourishment and development of their own capabilities to the fullest extent possible. Besides, not only the organisations but the individual organisational members also require coping strategies to deal with their respective environments.

Life in organisations is tough. Each working day in the organisation brings with it unprecedented tensions, expectations, conflicts and stresses arising out of organisational goals, current and expected individual performances, rewards and punishments and the resultant morale. It is crucial that an individual should be able to maintain his productivity, creativity, innovativeness and mental health on a continual basis to be able to achieve his own personal goals and organisational goals simultaneously.

This chapter presents a brief overview of some of the coping strategies for the individuals.

Transaction Analysis (TA)

It is often difficult for many of us to decipher the behaviour of others. The same individual appears to act totally differently in different situations, as if more than one personality had been superimposed over each other and different personality appeared on different occasions. Transaction Analysis, developed by Erice Berne, provides a very interesting insight into these behaviour patterns and helps obtain a clearer understanding of why we behave as we behave. Getting to know this may not eliminate erratic behavioural patterns but can certainly help in recognising them and controlling them to some extent.

A transaction is the unit of social intercourse. If two or more persons encounter each other, sooner or later one of them would speak or give some or other indication of acknowledging the presence of others. This is called transaction stimulus. Another person will say or do something which is in some way related to the above stimulus; that is called transaction response. Transaction analysis is the method of analysing transactions and arriving at conclusions about the reasons of occurrence of such transactions.

According to TA, everyone has three typical modes of behaviour. They are called the parent ego state, the adult ago state and child ego state (P, A and C). By examining the stimulus and the response amongst a set of transactions between two persons, one can identify the originating ego state for each of the persons.

The development of the concepts of P, A and C ego states is based on Dr. Penfield's experiments, in which he discovered that the parent and child are permanent recordings in the brain of a human being, having been formed at an impressionable age of 3 to 5 years, and incorporating both visuals and feelings. The adult ego state develops later in life and corresponds to mature, emotionless behaviour pattern.

The parent ego state represents 'taught' behaviour and incorporate the attitudes of self-righteousness, know-it-all, and superiority. This state is characterised by emotional, especially, anger feelings. The child ego state on the other hand represents emotional, impulsive behaviour, taking shape out of the frustrations, curiosities and raw feelings of the childhood. This can also be deemed as 'felt' behaviour. The Adult ego state represents information processing, logical and rational behaviour and can also be deemed as 'thought' behaviour.

When a person begins transactions with others, he assumes one out of three positions, which might be dominating at a given time, and may direct the transaction towards the same or another ego state of the other person. If the response to this transaction is in parallel to the first transaction, both together are called complementary transactions.

Example

(P)	(P)	1.	I want you to come to me immediately. Come quick.
(A)	(A)		
(C)	(C)	2.	Yes Sir, Sure !
(P)	(P)	1.	What is the time by your watch?
(A)	(A)		
(C)	(C)	2.	It is 4 p.m.

The complementary transactions are simple and conflict free. They can be perpetuated indefinitely because both the persons develop a compatibility.

Very often, however, the transactions are crossed. This happens when a stimulus transaction is addressed to one ego state but is responded to by a different ego state. The response transaction negates the sought for behavioural pattern and leads to a stoppage of further transactions.

Example

P	O	O	P	1.	Can you please come and see me?
A	O	O	A	2.	What do you think I am? Your servant?
C	O	O	C		

Another type of transaction is what is called a duplex transaction. In this type of transaction, there is a message at an explicit, social level, which is typically from one Adult to another Adult ego state; however, this message is accompanied by an underlying, psychological transaction which may have different interpretation altogether. These duplex transactions are also called games. Eric Bernes, the author of 'Games People Play' has identified "several such games at the psychological level."

Each of the ego states can be recognised by unique voice tones, types of words used, postures, facial expressions and body gestures.

Transaction analysis is an excellent method for introspection. It indicates whether one's behaviour is adult/parent/childlike most of the time. This is not to say that the behaviour should be adult all the time, for in that case the life would be dull and insipid. Parent and child ego states also have relevance, provided they don't dominate the transactions most of the time.

TA does not provide solutions *per se*, but the inferences drawn from TA can be helpful for any individual to modify his behaviour in the right direction.

Counselling

Managing people requires specialised skills. One such skill is the ability to provide counselling to the employees. A counsellor is a professional friend who helps people to solve their own problems and develop their latent potential, leading them to be winners. Counselling may be provided by the manager himself or by a professional counsellor. Sometimes, a manager concerned with one group/department may act as a counsellor for employees of another group/department, thus providing a degree of delinkage from the routine official work and official relationships.

Counselling is necessary when a person is bothered or dissatisfied with something, as a result of which his work performance is affected. This deterioration in work performance may be seen in terms of low motivation, reduced communication, too many mistakes etc. It is important to recognise the symptoms of such subordinate problems, get them resolved and make the subordinates productive. Counselling would help in getting the subordinate solve his problem. The problem itself may not be very clear and may be unarticulated. Further, it may not be possible for the subordinate to share his problem with others. As a result, the existence of a problem is manifested through certain clues, such as, sulking, avoiding meeting, looking depressed, being sarcastic or aggressive etc. Sometimes, the problem may be ventilated through expression of a feeling of frustration, anger or helplessness.

Counselling typically requires a counselling session between the counsellor and the counsellee. A counselling session has to be conducted in a relaxed atmosphere so that discussions can take place in a free, open and trusting manner. The aim of counselling session is not to solve the problem of the counsellee but to aid the counsellee in his problem solving. Through the counselling session, valuable insight is gained about the needs, potentialities, interests, difficulties and constraints, if any, of the counsellee. The counsellor acts as a professional in the counselling session and not as a personal friend.

The conduct of counselling session requires adoption of certain guidelines, which help in enhancing the utility of the counselling session. Firstly, comments or questions put up by the counsellor to the counsellee should be so designed as to help to counsellee think the matter through for himself, recognise his own feelings in the situation, accept his reactions and visualise the results of his action. Secondly, a non-judgemental posture should be adopted by the counsellor. Lastly, the counsellor should evoke trust of the counsellee, he should not only be seen to be a person with warmth and love, but also who can give an objective viewpoint. However, the counsellor should make clear that the responsibility for problem solving and growing lies with the counsellee only.

There is no harm in the manager assuming the role of a counsellor. However, he should undertake counselling only if he has a genuine interest in the development of subordinates. He should be genuinely willing to 'work' with the subordinate, provide him a caring and friendly atmosphere for counselling and keep the task relationship out of the picture. However, if the manager has some personal expectations regarding the outcome of the session, he would be subjectively involved and the counselling session is not likely to be successful.

An effective counsellor, whether a manager or a separate professional, is required to possess certain qualities. For instance, he should be mature and caring and willing to invest time and energy. He should be tactful and sensitive to the feelings and attitudes of the counsellee. He should display calmness and patience and should be a good listener. Above all, he should have a positive attitude towards human beings and should appear to be capable of helping the counsellee solve his problem. He should have the power of observation and remembering details and facts.

Team Building

Team building is a coping strategy aimed at increasing trust, improving communications and enhancing mutual acceptance amongst organisational members. The objective of team building is to make the group more cohesive and to remove impeding conditions and processes which interfere with the achievement of organisational goals by the group. Team building also endeavours towards resolution of conflicts amongst organisational members. One essential output of team building interventions is the sharing of leadership function by the manager with other team members.

A team is a group of people who rely upon group collaboration to experience success and goal achievement. Hawthrone experiments were the first to throw light on the team building concept, team spirit and the effect of team manager's attitude on team spirit. The works of McGregor, Likert, Blake and Mouton and others provided further concepts and empirical support for the team building intervention.

Unity of purpose is the main factor contributing to the development of highly efficient management team. Besides, it is important that managers should learn to cope with a totality of people under their direction and not merely on a one to one basis. A team draws upon strengths and experiences in several areas which should be effectively blended together for achieving group objectives.

Team building intervention becomes necessary when organisational output is below a desired level due to lack of team effort. This may be the result of unsatisfactory organisational processes as indicated by absenteeism, turnover etc. However, team building intervention may not be necessary if collaborative effort is not required, current level of communication and interactions is adequate and if planning, problem solving and decision making don't require co-ordination amongst members.

Lack of team spirit and cohesiveness is the result of several factors acting in unison with each other. These factors include, for instance, role ambiguity poor communication and lack of agreement on goals amongst the team members. Further, if certain members perceive that their contribution to the goals of the team is not matched by proportionate rewards, it may adversely affect their ability to act as members of a team. Another reason for low cohesiveness is insufficient sharing of commitment to a way of doing things.

It is essential that the value system of team members have a high degree of commonality, if the team has to be cohesive. For instance, there should be a more or less commonality of approach amongst team members on issues such as urgency of dealing with a problematic situation, degree to which the situation should be resolved, relative input that each member may have in taking decision, degree of rationality to be applied for in arriving at solution to the problem and relative importance attached to satisfying or optimising. Another issue on which a common understanding amongst team members is required, is the style of decision making and the degree of participation required for the same.

Team building intervention requires development of several related skills. These include the skills of self-understanding, understanding individual team members, understanding the team as a unit and developing team communication. For acquiring these skills, it is essential that the team leader has the qualities of honesty and trustworthiness, openness, growth orientation and respectfulness in communications.

There exist several models of team development. These include the goal setting model, the interpersonal model, the role model and the managerial grid model. The goal setting model involves joint participation of the team members in goal setting; this raises the level of commitment and motivation to achieve goals. In the interpersonal mode, the main objective is to increase the level of mutual trust/confidence and openness among members and to create an environment in which conflict is resolved, problems are solved and good decisions are made. In the role model, the team members strive to discuss and clarify their roles, both prescribed and discretionary and gain insight into leadership factors and interpersonal/intergroup relations. The managerial grid model is directed at 'corporate excellence rubric' which includes increasing managerial competence, and enriching capabilities of all members to contribute to solving problems and achieving organisational objectives.

The process of team building involves problem identification, diagnosis, developing solutions, preparing action plans for implementing solutions, training and control. Team building takes time; the action plans for team building should be periodically evaluated and updated. Team building intervention should ensure prior support from the top management team of the organisation.

Psychotherapy, Psychoanalysis and Psychiatric Interventions

These coping strategies are directed at the individual's psychology and aim at reorienting the behaviour of the individual towards a more integrated and harmonious pattern. These are based on the concepts of psychoanalysis mooted by Freud and further refinements carried over them in due course, by others.

Psychotherapy consists of an interaction between two individuals. One of the individuals is seeking help for a problem and is thus a patient. The other individual is the therapist who supposedly has the training and the resources to help the disturbed client. The first organised system of psychotherapy was psychoanalysis practised by Freud himself. Based on his experience with previous therapeutic procedures, Freud believed that even what appeared as successful attempts at removing the patient's symptoms would be of short duration and other substitute symptoms would subsequently appear. He felt that the underlying unconscious conflict was the real problem and until this was discussed and resolved, no lasting improvement would result. Since, the ideas and strivings that the individual repressed initially were very painful to him, they could not be expected to be easily brought forth by him.

Freud devised and adopted the Free Association method. In this method, the client is requested to lie down on a couch with the analyst sitting at the back and outside the direct line of vision. The client is instructed to release and allow his thoughts to flow freely, verbalising whatever occurs to mind. It is hypothesised that in such a relaxed state, the client might more freely verbalise his associations and eventually this may lead to the inner/repressed problem areas. As therapy progresses, the relationship between analyst and client deepens and certain characteristic patterns of response to the therapist are manifested.

The timing and accuracy of interpretation in psychoanalysis have been significant issues. It is believed that an accurate and well timed interpretation is useful therapy, whereas inaccurate and premature interpretation is likely to be non-constructive, retarding or sometimes harmful to the patient. Two important components of the result of psychoanalysis are attaining of the insight and working through. The insight refers to an understanding by the patient of his underlying difficulties. This is not attained in a dramatic aha or eureka manner, rather the patient accepts the insights only after a repetitive learning process. The knowledge gained through the process of psychoanalysis has to be worked through and assimilated.

As mentioned earlier, psychoanalysis was the first truly systematic form of psychotherapy. Subsequently, some modifications in the procedure took place and changes also occurred in the theoretical views and emphasis. Many basic postulates of Freud were adhered to by a class of physiotherapists, designated as 'psychodynamic'. These include concepts of repressed unconscious conflicts, transference, resistance, interpretation and insight. Another class of therapists known as electric therapists have also used some of the above concepts.

Case Rogers developed his own approach of psychotherapy, called client centred psychotherapy. This is a non-directive type of psychotherapy in which the analyst's expert role is curtailed.

Among the more recent contributions to the field of psychotherapy is that emerging from behavioural and cognitive orientations. Derived initially from the work of Pavlov on conditioning and learning theory, the behavioural approach has been the most important recent development in psychotherapy. This appears to be based on concepts which are rather the opposite of those advanced by the psychodynamic therapists.

Psychiatric intervention is a kind of emerging service in which psychotherapic resources must be mobilised immediately to be provided to the patients in situations where serious psychiatric consequences can occur if the treatment is delayed. The crisis therapist is trained to deal with acute psychiatric emergencies.

The psychiatric emergencies result from situations in which general functioning has been severely impaired and the patient is rendered incompetent or incapable of assuming personal responsibility. Obviously, this is a difficult crisis to handle as there is a greater urgency for understanding the situation in depth and beginning effective treatment. Fortunately, informants with some knowledge of the situation accompany or bring such patients foı treatment. The intervention involves assessment of the patient's psychological condition quickly, clarifying the situation that led to the present condition, mobilising mental health resources and arranging for follow-up to ensure continuity of treatment.

Psychotherapy and psychiatric interventions border on medical and health care support to the organisational personnel. They are thus coping strategies of the extreme kind, available to individuals who have been experiencing considerable stresses owing to job related conflicts.

Sensitivity Training

Sensitivity training/laboratory method is an instrument of organisation development, which has been practised and tested for decades to improve the human qualities of the organisation person. It works because it gives greater self-awareness. The effort here is to appreciate this coping strategy (reading what is being said should not serve as an encouragement to become an amateur sensitivity trainer).

Sensitivity training helps a person to register his internal needs, and values and recognise the way he perceives. It also helps the person to examine his inner world and look at his resources. When this is coupled with better reality perception, with the opportunities and expectations of the world outside his person, a case is made out for an appropriate integration of the two. This method assumes that the whole process can be better brought about by participation. This enables self-discovery and better diagnosis of people, processes and situations. Practitioners of this method would like to believe that, as a result, greater sensitivity is brought about. Sensitivity encourages growth and the result is a positive change.

It needs to be cautioned that sensitivity training has at times, perhaps, because of being handled wrongly, has caused problems of integration between the individual's and organisation's ratings of the individual competencies. Like everything else, used properly it helps, but a careless use would complicate and confuse.

Concluding Comment

The coping strategies described in this chapter are significant OD efforts requiring intervention of OD practitioners. To be effective, it is important that the support of top management be elicited and obtained. The choice of appropriate strategies depending upon the unique features of the organisation is crucial since, a wrong choice may lead only to a wastage of resources and may actually be counter-productive.

These coping strategies are not panacea for all organisational malaise. They are helpful up to a point and are not substitutes for common sense and the art of management which all managers in the organisation are expected to possess.

Chapter 8

Coping Strategies: Organisational

As pointed out in chapter 2, organisations continually interact with their environments. The environments are characterised by a high degree of variety and complexity. The organisations can survive and grow, if and only if, they are able to match their own varieties with that of their environment. This requires that way and means are found to enhance the capabilities of the organisations to effectively deal with their multifaceted environment. This dealing with the environment is not merely a defensive posture, but also includes developing capabilities to outsmart the environmental threats and challenges and convert them into opportunities. An effective organisation has the capabilities of converting every disadvantage into an advantage. Developing these capabilities requires use of various coping strategies which provide the ability to the organisations to 'cope' with their environment appropriately.

The coping strategies, such as, Technology Assessment and Diversification are concerned with the issues of business decisions by the organisation. Design intervention as a coping strategy is concerned with organisation structures. Management by objectives (MBO) another coping strategy used by the organisations, relates to structure, process and behavioural dimensions of organisations. Systems Integration as a coping strategy is concerned with structure and processes in organisations. Training is a coping strategy, primarily concerned with the structural and behavioural dimensions of the organisation. Lastly, Action Learning is concerned with the behavioural dimension.

This chapter discusses the key features of the above mentioned coping strategies, their merits and demerits, and their efficacy in providing the coping ability to organisations.

Technology Assessment

Technology has a key role to play in enabling an organisation to perform its functions and achieve its objectives. The introduction of new technologies in execution of various operations in its functional areas helps an organisation to derive the advantages of better quality and functionality of its products, high productivity of operations and cost-effectiveness. Technology provides the organisation a competitive advantage and in turn helps achieve higher profitability and growth.

However, no technology provides the cutting edge to an organisation for all time to come. Innovations take place continually and technological obsolescence starts taking place sooner than later. A continual process of technology assessment becomes crucial to enable an organisation update its technology from the right source at the right time.

Technology assessment involves an audit of existing technologies, identification of the needs for induction of new technologies, forecasting the scenario for technological changes outside the organisation in the short-term and long-term, selection of appropriate technology for induction in the organisation in the future and planning for technology transfer. The decision to introduce the selected technology is accompanied by an examination of the work design management of the change process, training in operation and maintenance of the new technology and other socio-technical issues such as displacement of labour, industrial relations problem etc.

Technology assessment requires a top level in an organisation. It requires an entrepreneurial approach, risk taking capabilities and an innovative culture. It requires the capabilities to look forward to the future and carefully scan the technology developments and sources thereof. It requires a considerable clarity of purpose and selection of appropriate criteria for carrying out technology assessment objectively and at a time when it is most needed.

Technology assessment as a coping strategy has long-term implications for the organisation. Given the nature of products and services produced by the organisation, its core technology does not change. However, technological advancements brought into the organisation with the help of this strategy can alter the work methods, information flows and job designs substantially. If imaginatively handled, technology assessment is an excellent coping strategy, which strikes at the core of business handling activities of the organisation.

Diversification

Diversification refers to addition of new products to the existing product line of an organisation. This is a coping strategy which helps the organisation adapt to its environment not by merely changing its structure but, by reorienting its functions and objectives. Diversification provides capabilities of better resource utilisation, synergy in operations, more effective control on resources available and products marketed and higher overall growth.

Diversification includes incremental additions to the existing product line as well as *de novo* identification of additional business. In the case of incremental additions to the existing product line, the existing technology, manpower and other resources are used with certain marginal changes to obtain outputs of the proposed additional products. However, for *de novo* additional line of business, new set of resources, facilities and equipment may have to be provided. In most cases, diversification my take place in the form of vertical integration, i.e. the new products are either the raw materials for the existing products or the higher end products/ services which can be produced with the help of current products/ services of the organisation. However, it is not uncommon for organisations to diversify into totally unrelated areas. In such cases, the single most important common factor between the existing and diversified business is the corporate identity of the organisation and all that goes with it.

Diversification, unlike technology assessment, is not a continual process. The need for diversification is perceived by the top management of the organisation as response to changes taking place in the outside world. A continual boundary spanning activity is required for an organisation to anticipate future changes in the nature of product and services demanded by the market. A review of its internal operations on a periodic basis helps the organisation to assess its strengths and weaknesses. Diversification as a coping strategy helps the organisation to build upon its strength and pick up the opportunities offered by the outside world, as sensed through its boundary spanning activities.

Diversification has long-term implications for the organisation. It requires commitment of organisational resources to newer areas and has an inherent risk taking element. It involves identification of alternatives and selection of the most appropriate diversification strategy, backed by careful analysis. It requires a clarity of purpose at the level of top management of the organisation and, more often than not, it leads to an irreversible decision for the organisation. Like in the case of technology assessment, diversification is an excellent coping strategy for the organisation, if carefully handled. The gap between the decision to diversify and to translate the decision into a reality has to be bridged by a long drawn process of preparing the organisation for change, smoothening out the rough edges of maladjustment and harnessing resources to achieve the requisite benefits.

Design Interventions

Technology assessment and diversification are almost invariably accompanied by design interventions to ensure that the structure of the organisation is appropriate for the technology and nature of business. It is obvious that the structure has to dovetail with the demands of technology, the product mix and the continual changes brought in by them. Besides, the structure has to provide the capabilities for carrying out the processes of technology assessment and boundary spanning. This requires the use of appropriate design interventions.

Design intervention as a coping strategy is important in its own right also, even when not seen in conjunction with technology assessment and diversification. An organisation failing to perform well for a long time is an automatic candidate for a design intervention. Sometimes, the change in top management team of an organisation warrants a corresponding structural change in the organisation. Attrition of key persons from the organisation, available indications of low morale and high employee turnover from the organisation or the occurrence of a catastrophic event provide other valid and significant reasons for design interventions.

Design interventions involve a careful analysis of the current tasks performed in the organisation, authority accountability relationships, communication and information flow, roles and responsibilities and current sources of conflict. These factors are judged in terms of their efficacy in meeting the long- and short-term objectives of the organisation. In addition, the thrust areas for the organisation are identified, as determined by the business policy, environmental constraints and top managements value systems. Attitude surveys, OD workshops or nominal group technique exercise may be conducted to obtain the perceptions of the organisational members on existing lacunae in structure and most desirable changes. These approaches, put together, provide the necessary directions for restructuring the organization.

Design intervention aims at fulfilling organisational goals relating to the three dimensions of organisational effectiveness simultaneously. These are the task dimension, the behavioural dimension and the adaptation dimension. The emerging structure would thus have the capabilities of achieving organisation's current objectives while ensuring that the organisational members have the requisite channels for motivation and growth and that organisation itself has the capabilities to adapt to the future technological and other environment changes.

It is almost impossible to carry out a design intervention without due regard to the existing personnel, their competence and their expectations from the organisation. Though conceptually, one would look for an 'objective' structure, it is not possible to wish away the existing organisational personnel, who must fit into the revised structure with all their infirmities.

Design intervention as a coping strategy has to be a constant feature of an organisation. No periodicity can be prescribed for when to go in for design interventions; it should be done as and when the situation warrants it.

Management by Objectives (MBO)

Management by objectives or MBO as it is more popularly known is another important coping strategy for the organisations. As the name suggests, the application of MBO requires formulation of objectives which are definite, clear and unambiguous and are available as standards of performance, references for control and guides for performance appraisals. These objectives are formulated in relation to the corporate business policy of the organisation and are typically arrived at through a joint process of objective setting between the manager and his subordinates.

The setting of objectives at various levels commences with the top management. The key result areas or effectiveness areas are identified for each managerial position in such a way that there are no overlaps in responsibilities and, at the same time, no responsibilities participatory, in which case the subordinates have enough leeway to influence the objectives being set; or it may be primarily based on directions from the top management with virtually no discretion with the subordinates to redefine/alter their objectives.

MBO may be linked with performance appraisals. The performance of organisational members is evaluated in terms of achievement of the objectives assigned to them earlier. Thus, the appraisal is result oriented rather than attribute or effort oriented.

An implicit assumption, perhaps axiomatic, in the MBO approach is that all actions are goal directed. However, many of the organisational personnel are not clear of their goals, thus losing the focus in their actions and consequently achieving a performance, which is definitely not the best. On the other hand, it is quite common for managers to have surplus goals which may be exogenous to the organisation system. The objectives in the MBO approach get evolved and clarified through a meticulous planning process, which therefore becomes the delivery mechanism for these objectives. Thus, the essential achievement of MBO is to transform statements of organisational purpose into concise operational objectives, plans and budgets.

It is important to emphasise that objectives must be acceptable to the people whose activities are involved; these must be attainable, motivational, simple and verifiable for periodic evaluation.

MBO requires, as a prerequisite, the knowledge of what is expected on the part of both manager and the subordinate. It also involves discussing the performance level achieved *vis-à-vis* the standards of performance. Such a feedback should be supportive, immediate, as individual as possible and should involve coaching or counselling as needed, to enhance learning. The review during the MBO process should primarily be a dialogue between manger and the subordinate and should focus only on performance improvement.

The MBO approach helps in uncovering problems of organisations on individual jobs, in particular units and in the company as a whole. It facilitates a high degree of self-control by individual managers and leads to better management by forcing managers to plan for results rather than merely activities. It forces managers to clarify organisational goals and structure and encourages people to commit themselves to their goals. It helps the organisation become better prepared in response to changing internal and external environment. It also helps reduce conflicts stemming from ambiguities in division of responsibility and authority. It helps people to get to know what is expected of them and leads to decreased need for personality appraisals.

However, critical references to the MBO approach abound in literature. MBO is seen by many critics as perpetuating the hostility between manager and the subordinate and intensifying the distrust. The whole process of MBO appears to be based on a short-term, egocentric perspective with a reward punishment psychology. The MBO process does not take into cognizance the personal goals of organisational members. If interests don't mesh, individuals begin to experience conflict. The pressure of suppressed wishes may become so heavy that the individual finally makes an impulsive break. Perhaps, MBO misses the human point altogether.

It is very difficult to sit upon judgement about whether MBO has the above shortcomings or not. One reason for this is that MBO, even in its concept form, has many shades and it means many things to many people. It can be deemed to be an effective method of management, a performance appraisal system, a motivation system or even a democratic way of organisational functioning. Apart from conceptual differences, there are variations in the ways MBO is implemented in organisations, leading to different, often mixed results. Yet, in a way this debate is redundant, because in which other way can one manage, except by objectives?

Obviously, MBO is a coping strategy for the organisations is significant, despite the debate that accompanies its theory and its implementation in the organisations.

Systems Integration

Systems integration may be defined as an approach to conceptualisation, design and problem solving which takes into account a holistic view of an activity and its context. The underlying assumption of this approach is that there is always a wider context in which a problem scenario should be looked at or a decision taken. For instance, in a multinational corporation, the top management at the headquarters can't and does not consider any single country's operations in isolation, while examining the impact of top level decision making. Similarly, a production manager can't look at the production problems in isolation but has to look at them in the wider context of the entire organisation including functions such as marketing, finance and industrial relations. Further, one Government department can't have a set of policies and programmes which are not consistent with the policies and programmes of other Government departments. These are illustrations of the systems integration approach in practice.

Conceptually, there is nothing new about the systems integration approach. As a coping strategy, it has been practised by organisations in their management functions, more or less as a common sense approach. (Of course, if the common sense is abdicated and decisions based on isolated cases are taken, as against holistic consideration of all factors concerned, the results are disastrous.) However, the recent advances in information technology have made this approach much more practicable than in the past. Information technology has dramatically increased the information flow amongst geographically dispersed parts of organisations and has led to the shrinking of time and distance. This has enabled mangers to look beyond the immediately visible organisational boundaries and enlarge their frames of reference.

Systems integration is attained in practice with the help of linkage provided by information flow across various subsystems of the organisation. Lack of or inadequate information flow results in loss of cohesiveness and thus, imposes constraints on attaining system integration. Thus, information is the weaving thread amongst all constituents of the organisation and the information flow needs to be nourished. In fact, an organisation system becomes a dynamic entity only by virtue of information flow amongst its constituents.

The adoption of systems integration approach by the managers is promoted by a positive attitude towards it, cultivated through training. Such a positive disposition makes the organisational members more open and amenable to widescoping of the context. The creativity of the human mind is at its best when such an openness is available. This creativity is further facilitated through interventions such as idea associations, cross-adaptation, experience sharing and action learning. (Action Learning is covered in the next chapter). Various group processes especially consensus methodologies help enhance human creativity and thereby the adoption of systems integration approach.

It is also observed that internal and external competition lead to an increasing pressure for systems integration. Both the types of competition compel the members, sooner or later, to explore avenues for joint survival. These avenues are available in managerial styles which bring in more cohesiveness in the organisation. The deviant members either opt out or reorient themselves to the needs of the organisation, provided, however, that there is a dynamic leadership in the organisation that ushers in the forces of integration and cohesiveness.

Concurrent with factors which promote systems integration, there exist several constraints to systems integration. Firstly, there are finite limits to the information processing capabilities of organisations or its members. A human being can't process more than five to nine chunks of information at one time. This severely constrains him in making use of all the information made available by the advents in information technology and leads to the possibility of taking non-informed decisions, despite availability of information. Lastly, the cost of information technology support for achieving systems integration can be prohibitive.

There is considerable potential for inculcating the systems integration approach amongst members of an organisation. A positive attitude towards and aptitude for systems integration can be developed through an organisation wide thrust. The philosophy of systems integration should permeate the value system of the organisation. This will help correcting the myopic, sub-optimisation approaches often resorted to by various members of organisation. Like any other OD approach, systems integration should start with the top management. It may or may not require intervention of an external consultant. Special laboratory exercises can be developed to facilitate learning of the basic concept of systems integration. However, attitudinal training towards systems integration requires well defined job design and information flows in the organisation as a precondition. Implementing systems integration approach requires the introduction of appropriate information technology as well as a cultural change in the organisation.

Training and Development

Another important coping strategy for organisations is training and development of organisational personnel. Training is a planned and systematic effort that helps in modifying or developing knowledge, skills and attitudes of the persons undergoing training. It provides a learning experience and helps in effective performance of an activity or range of activities. Thus, training facilitates adequate handling of jobs in any work situation.

In many instances, training is dismissed as an activity that merely has a cost associated with it; what is overlooked is that the cost of not having training could be much higher to the organisation in terms of inefficient and low productivity operations owing to lack of adequate training. It is also to be emphasised that training is not an end itself; rather it is means to an end. Therefore, it is essential that the effectiveness of training be continually evaluated.

Training and learning are two sides of the same coin and go hand in hand. Learning process is not only for those who get training but also for those who give training. Again, it is often seen that training is designed in accordance with the knowledge and skills of the trainers and not according to the needs for training of the learners. However, it is important that training should be learner oriented and not trainer oriented.

There are significant differences between training and education. While education has a general domain, is growth oriented and has a long-term impact, training has a specific domain, is job oriented and has a short-term impact. Further, education usually has a broad coverage and results in considerable variability in learning. Training typically has a more focused coverage and results in a greater uniformity in learning. Both training and education along with action learning are the three important, interdependent sources for promoting learning and development.

Systematic training involves four key activities following a cyclic process. To begin with, training needs should be identified for the targeted groups of organisation personnel. This requires consideration of several factors such as standards of performance on the job, current status of the knowledge, skills and attitudes of the concerned personnel, target population profile, formulation of training objectives and motivational aspects influencing learning. The training activity should be designed on the basis of the identified training needs. A pilot training to test the training package developed should be attempted and the training design modified, if necessary. The other important activities are actually conduct of the training programme and assessment of the effectiveness of training, both through internal validation by the group of trainees as well as through external monitoring of training.

One type of analysis which can be carried out to decide the need for and to identify training needs is known as DIF Analysis. This analysis involves asking three types of questions; these are:

(a) Is the task difficult?
(b) Is the task important?
(c) Is the task frequent?

The need for and nature of training required to be provided for a given task is based on answers to the above questions.

The roles of a trainer are manifold. Firstly, he acts as a trainer in terms of actually carrying out training and assisting the trainee to earn. He is also a provider since, he designs training and thus, provides training packages. He is also a provider in terms of providing training to the trainers. His third role is similar to that of a consultant; he may advise the management on training policies being followed. A trainer is also an innovator, since, he solves performance problems of the organisation and supports the organisation to bring about change. Last but not the least, a trainer may also be a manager. In this role, he plans the training activities and monitors and controls the performance of training function *vis-à-vis* targets.

Certain assertions about training are worth reiterating. Training is an activity encompassing all states of life cycle. It is a continual process and is unidirectional. However, training is not a panacea; it may sharpen the potential and put a constraint on undesirable traits, but it can't provide something which does not exist.

Training as a coping strategy for organisations has a very important role to play in terms of developing human resources and making them capable of performing their roles appropriately in accordance with the needs of the organisation.

Action Learning

Action learning is perhaps the oldest concept in the encyclopaedia of organisational coping strategies. A look at the proverbs of any culture shows the meaning and wisdom of action learning. Did someone say it was learning by doing? Look before you leap, taught the grandma and two heads are better than one, taught the distraught mother. The growing person absorbed it and learnt it. The credit for recognising the relevance of this mode of learning in organisational context is, however, by convention, ascribed to R.W. Revans. Beginning from early 1970s, it has become a much wanted tool to attack problems to which there are no known answers. In other words, when there is a problem and there is no known answer, learning through action is required.

Action learning is not useful for puzzles. It is useful to respond to the classical questions such as who knows about this problem, who cares about it and who can do anything about it. This paradigm brings like minded people together in a project format and poses the questions such as what are we trying to do, what is stopping us from doing it and what might we be able to do without it. Action learning does not end with a reporting of the first round of answers to these questions. The solutions are taken back to where the problem is, applied, tested and results brought back to the group. The iteration continues till the problem is solved. Perhaps, quoting Revans would be only fair to the person who has done so much to popularise this coping strategy. He says, "If I want to help a manager know something that is to do something better, I try to help him find out what he is doing now and get him to improve it." The practice of action learning is not without its share of pathos. Like all mortals, he laments what he does not approve. His regret is perhaps best reflected in a quotation from an unknown source:

> "The clever man will tell you what he knows, he may even try to explain it to you. The wise man encourages you to discover it for yourself, even though he knows it inside out. But since he seems to give you nothing, we have no need to reward him. Thus the wise have disappeared and left in a desolation of the clever."

Concluding Comments

The coping strategies presented in this chapter are not the only ones known. However, they represent all important types of interventions. They look like assorted approaches for enhancing organisational effectiveness, each with different focus. Further, they are not substitutes but are supplementary to each other. However, it is important that a right selection of the coping strategies is made by the top management, keeping in view the unique organisational features, availability of appropriately skilled OD practitioners and past experiences with adoption of coping strategies.

An Overview of the Following Case on Action Learning

The following case on action learning vividly illustrates the potential of this important organisational coping strategy. What is most fascinating about this case is that the organisation and its chief executive, an interview with whom has been presented, don't have a blind faith in this OD strategy or in any other OD strategy, for that matter. They believe in no rigid paradigms of success, nor do they get bogged down by the semantics. They believe in the philosophy of learning through action and practise this philosophy all the time.

Can one really learn action learning by reading about action learning? The answer is both yes and no. Reading about it as in the text earlier and as in the case following, is helpful in understanding its basics. However, the proof of the pudding lies in the eating. Why not just start practising action learning in your organisation and watch its success? And remember, you don't have to call it 'action learning'.

The student readers can also practise action learning while studying the subject of OD. Why not get into action straightaway? Identify at least one more organisation which practises action learning or is very close to it and makes out a case which can be shared with your fellow readers.

Action Learning in Practice at Organisation XYZ

One organisation in India, which has been practising Action Learning quite successfully is analysed below by way of a conversation with its C.E.O. The organisation for various reasons is just referred to as XYZ and its chief as C.E.O. Ltd. The authors interviewed Chief Executive of the organisation to know more about the way Action Learning is understood and practised there. Here are some excerpts from the interview.

Question: We understand that you have pioneered the use of Action Learning approach for solving many organisational problems at your organisation, could you kindly tell us about the concept of Action Learning as understood and practised by you?

The CEO: Thanks for complimenting us for successfully practising the approach of action learning. Let me, however, begin by saying that we have been practising action learning without really calling it so. Our experience has been that names alienate people. What is important is that the basic tenets of action learning are recognized and made use of.

The first and foremost tenet of action learning is that there are no set formulae for success. The paradigms of success change very fast. If one strategy has given successful results at some time, it is quite likely that the same strategy may not work in the future. It is therefore essential to question all the assumptions and not to take any strategy, any success formula for granted.

The ability of an organisation to become open to such questioning comes through encouraging free communication. The organisation should strive to form problem solving groups which "naturally question", and the contributions of such groups should be used to the advantage of the organisation. The freedom and questioning power given to such a group ensures that nothing is considered sacrosanct. As Revans, the profounder of Action Learning asserts, if you attack everything that is sacred, the problem becomes more and more transparent; therefore, it is important not to believe in any fixed patterns.

The managers in business organisations typically envision role models for success and look down upon the subordinates, since these subordinates do not fit into the role models of success. In this process, what is forgotten is that most of the new ideas come from the younger lot of people.

Question: Would you care to give some illustrations of the use of Action Learning approach at the organisation you head?

The CEO: I would like to share our experience of using Action Learning approach for making a conscious shift in the customer profile of our company. Initially, the cement industry contributed over 60 per cent to the business, as it was the major user of the power control systems manufactured by us. In fact, there was so much business in the cement and related industries in the year 1987 that one would have thought that this was a clear path to pursue. However, we were continually on the look out for enlarging our customer profile. In 1987-88, we used the concepts of action learning and identified metal industry as a potential customer base. We discovered that though the language used by cement and the metal industry was different in essence both the industries looked for a similar product. In 1989, a big slump in the cement industry was witnessed; however, by then we had already switched the application of our knowledge base from cement to the metal industry and the shift in our customer profile had materialized.

I would like to mention here that for complex issues relating to corporate strategy, action learning alone is not enough. Often, this approach has to be supplemented with analytical tools which would help structure the problem. In fact, we have found that the Analytical Hierarchy Process (AHP) has blended very well with action learning. We have developed an approach called HAALP, which has come as a result of the blending of AHP and Action Learning. However, as I said earlier, the names of the techniques are not important, what is important is the use of the techniques.

Another example, I would like to give, relates to the revision in the layout of production area of our company. Before the Action Learning intervention, the production area was very congested; however, we were able to develop a revised layout which provided substantial free space even with a 20 to 30 per cent increase in the volume of production. This successful intervention was to a great extent dependent upon the Japanese concept of "GO to GAMBA" (Gamba means a workplace), i.e. the right place to solve a problem is the place of action itself.

To give a more practical shape to action learning, we have formed innovative action groups in our company. One of them is QUEST (Quality Excellence and Customer Satisfaction through Teaming), which as the name suggests is concerned with meeting the quality expectations of customers. The second group called "Pathfinders", on the other hand, is an action group, engaged primarily in solving internal problems.

We have also set up at our office premises, a special room called IGNITE (Idea Generation for Innovation and Teaming). The employees use this room for engaging in self-study and come out with new and innovative ideas on their own which are subsequently highlighted in the room. Sometimes, the words of the employees are encouraged to contribute ideas for promoting excellence, the ideas generated are prominently displayed. Besides, anyone who does anything excellent in any forum is given recognition. These kinds of things make our company a lively place to work at.

Question: Did you at any stage experience any difficulties or even failure in adopting the action learning approach?

The CEO: My experience is that the biggest enemy to the success of action learning or any other intervention, for that matter, is cynicism, which needs to be broken. Budgetary constraints often pose another major block because it may not be possible to implement the ideas generated through action learning owing to financial difficulties. For instance, we had an environmental overhaul project evolved through the action learning approach, which required an investment of Rs. 70 to 80 lakhs.

Since, it was not possible to make such a large investment in one go, we felt that it will be a good idea to divide this project into three phases. We explained this constraint to the group and got the suggestion of phasing accepted by the group members.

A problem can often arise when the top people in the organisation inadvertently impose their will, against the deliberations of an action learning group. We had this difficulty for instance, in insisting on buying a particular brand of computer hardware and a business software product, which were later found to be unsuitable for the organisation.

Question: Is action learning, in your opinion, suitable to all types of organisations?

The CEO: It is important to recognize that action learning can raise the level of conflict in the organisation It is, therefore, most suited to organisations which are in a perpetual stage of conflict and chaos and which take conflict in their stride or rather, where conflict is constructively used for an advantage by the organisation. On the other hand, for an organisation where harmony is important and which believes in peaceful adventureless co-existence, action learning may not be suitable.

In fact, I recall that one of my colleagues from our parent company in America recently visited India and was an observer in the annual budget formulation exercise being carried out by a group of managers at our company. He was shocked to watch the heated arguments and the apparent acrimony they generated and felt that the meeting was degenerating and becoming counter-productive. However, he was pleasantly surprised to see the very same people interacting amicably in the evening get-together. Apparently, the conflict was a part and parcel of the idea generation process and had nothing to do with personal relationships.

However, coming back to the type of organisations where action learning is more relevant I feel that high technology organisations, organisations facing competitive pressure, organisation with high professional to administrative staff ratio and organisations with limited hierarchies will be able to successfully use action learning. On the other hand, organisations where hierarchy becomes more or less synonymous with feudalism and where dissent is discouraged will not find any use for action learning.

Chapter 9

Information Technology and Organisations

The importance of information in an organisation cannot be over-emphasized. Information flows within an organisation and between the organisation and its external environment have existed ever since the organisation came into existence. Information is generated whenever anything happens (or does not happen). The availability of information influences the process of decision making at various levels of management. These decisions, in turn, lead to actions, which again generate new information. Thus, actions, information and decision making continually form a cyclic pattern. While this pattern has been in existence since ages, the almost instantaneous generation, transmission, processing and flow of information has been enabled by what we call Information Technology (IT).

This unprecedented acceleration in the pace of generation and sharing of information has incredible implications for the organisations. Not only have the organisational processes such as communication, co-ordination and decision making been totally transformed, even the organisation structures have undergone major changes. IT has led organisations to redefine their business purpose, rethink their product and services offerings to their customers, seek newer methods for obtaining competitive advantage, and develop newer paradigms of effectiveness. In other words, organisations have reinvented themselves, faced as they are with fundamental and revolutionary impact of IT.

The scope of the term IT has also undergone unrecognisable change over the decades. The basic essence of IT remains as information acquisition, processing, transmission, storage and retrieval. However, the modes through which this happens have been transformed. The word "Internet", for instance, was non-existent in the literature of late eighties and early nineties; but the mid-nineties have ushered in the internet revolution, now bringing in its fold new forms or organizations called dotcom organizations, new ways of doing business called e-commerce, and new ways of government called e-governance. These revolutionary changes are relegating almost everything else forming part of erstwhile IT into the background. The basic premise that IT reflects the convergence of computer and communication technologies remains unaltered, yet this convergence has much bigger meaning than indicated – the convergence now implies an almost total fusion of the technologies and product of information, communications and entertainment (ICE), creating global impacts. It may sound like a 'clichè', but is truce that IT has created a new information society, thereby also leading to increased complexity facing the organisations.

The revolutionary changes in IT have given pre-eminence to the role of knowledge in modern-day organizations. Obviously, knowledge has a much large spectrum than information. Knowledge includes data, information, interpretation of the information and derivation of new meanings and newer insights from such interpretation. The explosion of content of the internet has led to availability to tones of ever-changing and ever-growing information, both relevant and often irrelevant, and has made the task of carving out knowledge from the heap of information a difficult art. It however demonstrates the capacity of IT to generate knowledge. Systematic IT interventions are now being increasingly adopted to acquire knowledge from customers, employees and other stakeholders in the organization, distribute this knowledge across the organization and leverage the knowledge in accordance with the strategic needs of the organization.

How has IT Evolved?

The IT of today is so different from its evolution that it is difficult to see much association between the two. The IT of the earliest era was typically seen in the form of mainframe computers based on vacuum tube technology, occupying immense space and consuming lot of energy for operation. The computing room was a sacred place with restricted entry. Batch processing of data dominated the computing scene, in which the priority for computer applications rested with the computer departments, more often glamorously designated as Electronic Data Processing (EDP) departments. No wonder, the power equations in a typical organization joining the bandwagon of computerization, clearly favoured this mighty group of people. As the merits of automation through computers became more widely known, the clamour for computerization accelerated and it became an inevitable requirement in business organizations gradually. The technology development process meanwhile led to development of increasingly more powerful, less energy consuming and smaller in size computing systems, based on transistor devices, and later, based on ICs and other digital electronic devices. The mainframe computer evolved into mini-computers, and in due course, into micro-computers. Steadily, the software component of IT became more and more critical in driving computing applications, and the relative proportion of hardware costs in the total computerised system cost rapidly declined.

The beginning of micro-computers also witnessed an exponential growth in the demand for computing power at the user end, rather than centralised at the so-called computer centres, where the users had little discretion on the how and why of jobs being executed. The increasing commercial availability of standardized IBM PCs and its compatibles all-over the world brought in the PC revolution, empowering the end-user with all the computing power available at the desktop. This, again, was the era when the Big Blue (IBM) misread the market and over-emphasised the mainframe, paying little attention to the PC. On the other hand, Bill Gates, the co-founder of Microsoft, saw the future of computing at this juncture, and through the now world-famous Microsoft products like MS-DOS and later MS WINDOWS, became virtually the biggest player in the computer market. No wonder, in due course, Bill Gates became the richest man of the world, but that is not important. What is important is that the immense power of computer was suddenly available directly to the end-user. This power only grew with time as the computer manufactures enhanced the hardware from PC to PC-XT to PC-AT. More and more of computer memory was made available, the storage capacity for computerised data was increased manifolds and newer software applications were developed at breakneck speeds. The computer user had never so good !

With the rapid advances in communication technologies and the need for on-line real time applications strongly emerging, a trend towards connectivity began and accelerated soon after. The batch processing era was overtaken by on-line processing era. The centralized processing system was supplemented by distributed data processing systems, wherever warranted by the needs of the computer applications. The need for Management Information Systems (MIS) for overall planning, monitoring and control of organisational operations got highlighted; the top and middle management level persons in organisations started demanding of computing power at their own desks. They brought in the era of computerised MIS, Decision Support Systems (DSS) and Executive Information Systems (EIS). The craving for simulating the human intelligence through computers led to the language processing. The shape of IT was rapidly changing !

The early era computing in organisations was dominated by simple applications such as payrolls, personnel, financial accounting, production and materials/inventory accounting, utility billing etc. In due course, word processing, spreadsheets and database management systems became the all pervasive applications. On the shop floor, the Computerised Numerically Controlled (CNC) machines were introduced, and Computer Aided Design (CAD) became a widespread application. Mass-customisation became a reality and a perfectly sensible concept on account of IT applications in manufacturing. The specialised management functions such as Materials and Production Management witnessed the introduction of Material Requirement Planning (MRP) and later the Enterprise Resource Planning (ERP), and even Integrated Supply Chain Management. The service industry such as airlines, hotels and even railways were IT enable to provide on-line reservation services; and banks brought in Automatic Teller Machines (ATMs) to provide new conveniences to their customers. For meeting the information and transactional needs of users on a variety of public utility related services, proprietary network in different sectors/industries were made available by entrepreneurs.

With a proliferation of IT all-over, and an increasing appreciation of the possibility of IT penetration in all facets of business, the era of IT-based services caught on. India as a country with a large pool of scientific manpower was able to develop highly skilled software engineers, dramatically illustrating the advent of a high revenue-generating line of business, namely, software services. Remote processing of data for backroom operations became a new trend with most international organisations like the airlines achieving economic advantages through such strategies. The consumer products of the modern era were enriched with smart applications, and the markets were privy to the availability of intelligent appliances, e.g. smart automobiles, washing machines with fuzzy logic etc. and even intelligent buildings. The difference between human and machine intelligence was rapidly narrowing down.

The above account of evolution in IT is neither comprehensive nor chronologically accurate, as its purpose is merely to highlight the sea changes that have taken place in the world of IT. But the story is only half complete. As if the above pace of accelerated development was not enough, the internet revolution of the nineties has brought in yet another major upheaval. The way we communicate with our customers, vendors, competitors and collaborators in business, has totally changed. E-mail and voice-mail through internet threaten to make postal and conventional telephony services obsolete. Thanks to this revolution, an organisation need no longer be formed out of brick and mortar—it can maintain only an electronic existence. Even a small tiny organisation can now become a global player, making all purchase, marketing and financial transaction through the net. With the rapid proliferation of websites on the internet, search engines and portals to facilitate systematic access of information have emerged. To handle the information explosion, a new class of service providers called "Infomediaries" have evolved, who play the role of intermediaries in generating and distributing information. The way we do business has transformed with the advent of E-commerce; the click of a mouse is enough to place and order for products and services from the grocery shop in one's own city or from a superstore in some distant part of the universe having a formidable presence on the net. Suddenly, new terms with profound meaning behind them, such as B2B, B2C, e-banking, virtual education, e-learning etc. have come in vogue. Data Mining, Customer Relationship Management (CRM) are some of the newly emerging concepts in marketing through the net.

It is obvious that IT of today is vastly different from that yesteryears in terms of the nature of equipment, applications and spread its impact. Significantly, the IT of tomorrow will be even different from that of today, and much rapid and extensive than in the past. The not-so-distant future will witness a convergence of interactivity, computing and entertainment, resulting in a virtual disappearance of distinction between, say, a TV, a mobile phone and a PC. More intelligent and smart devices and appliances are bound to penetrate the office and the home. The people in the future organisation are naturally going to find themselves in a much more IT-savvy organization culture than at present.

IT and Organisation Structures

In his famous book, "Future Shock" (1973), Alvin Toffler had observed that "today's business environment, convulsing with surprises, upsets, reversals and generalised turbulence, has necessitated, and is consequently leading to major changes in the structuring of business organisations". He had coined novel terms such as the "emergence of Flexi-firm", the "demassification of organisation structures", replacement of the uniform structure of a firm by a diversity of organisational arrangements, "rebuilding of business organisations on post-bureaucratic lines" and "decolonisation of organisation". It is difficult to assess the degree to which such prophecies have been realised, because the nature of change have varied across types of organizations. While the Government-owned or monopolistic organisations have been somewhat immune from such changes, those in the thick of competition have come fairly close to the never structural configurations. The on-slaught of downsizing, described as business process reengineering in a technical parlance, has trimmed many organisation world-over, the experience of which has not always been happy for the individuals concerned. However, from the point of view of being effective and responsive, these structural changes have yielded the desired results. Networking of people, irrespective of whether they are technically in the same organisation or belong to different organisations, is increasingly becoming the norm. Boundaries, say between the vendors and the organisation, or say, between the organisation and its customers are increasingly becoming only notional. The blurring of time and space brought about by modern day communication devices and technologies, such as e-mail, mobile phone and internet-enabled cellular systems has brought in yet another dimension of complexity into organisation structure. The geography just does not matter any more; the modern organisation has indeed become seamless and omniscient.

It is interesting to recall the interesting debates in the organisation literature on the impact of IT on centralisation and decentralisation in organisations. It was vociferously argued by one school of thought that IT promotes centralisation, while an equally strong position taken by others was that IT promotes decentralisation in organisation. The subsequent views reported in the literature tended to take more balanced and realistic positions. It was stated that there is no inherent relationship between IT and decision authority structure, and that IT is a malleable tool which can be used to achieve what is intended to be achieved in terms of decision authority structure. The evidence on the ground suggests that there has been a mixed pattern on this account. Emergence of large multinational organisations with centralised policy-making, environment scanning and overall co-ordination functions, has substantiated the centralisation capabilities of IT. The fact that the gross sales revenue of selected MNCs is even higher than the GDP of some countries is quite revealing. On the other hand, the prescriptions like "Think Globally and Act Locally" and their increasing acceptance in the corporate world, reflect the importance of adaptation according to local requirements, which can be best achieved only in decentralised mode. Both these tendencies appear to co-exist in accordance with the needs of the organisation.

In this context, it is worthwhile looking at the model of an organization as an agency relationship built on a set of contracts among self-interested agents. In the decentralized mode, an organization would allow more and more decision making done by the agents, while in the centralised mode, more and more decisions will be taken by the principal, upwards in the hierarchy. The risk in decentralised decision making is the likely goal divergence between the principal and the agents, while in the centralized decision making, the costs associated with processing information upwards in the hierarchy can be high. While considering the impact of IT, it is observed that owing to its ability to provide improved monitoring and performance evaluation capabilities to the principal. It can promote decentralization. Interestingly, the argument can be turned upside down, and it can be said that IT also promotes centralization by improving the quality and speed of information processing. In actual practice, an organization may use IT to decentralize some decision making and centralise some others, leading to a hybrid structure.

The network organization, described as the "structural imperative of information age", is a newly emerging structural configuration. In this, the various organizational members work together in loosely interconnected ventures, forming part of the total organisation and enabling it to provide a quick, flexible and strategic response to the environment. The network organization embodies the principle of free enterprise into the organization by providing a unique blend of control and freedom. The network working often extends from within the organization to between organizations, leading to an eventual blurring of organizational boundaries. Another perspective of network organization is the superimposition of the traditional functional hierarchy by informal, cross-functional networks. The traditional hierarchy is concerned with routine operations, and the network is an enabling mechanism for flexible and responsive decision making by the organization in the complex environment surrounding it. IT provides the requisite communication and coordination system and extended integration amongst diverse elements. The networks create market-like structures inside an organisation, providing platforms for idea and information sharing, joint strategizing collaboration amongst diverse organizational entities. They also result in the emergence of team-based, problem-focused and often-changing work groups supported by rich electronic communications.

IT and Business Strategy

The fact that IT can be a key driver of business strategy has long been recognized. It has been realized that IT is not merely a tool for number crunching and increasing office productivity, and that IT can even help shape the business strategy of an organisation. An evidence of organisations discovering the strategic importance of IT comes from the fact that the brick and mortar companies are increasingly reincarnation themselves as dotcom companies, or at least creating an on-line personality of themselves, in addition to their conventional physical existence. The very products and services which many of the companies offer today are inconceivable in isolation of IT. One can't visualise, for instance, Yahoo or Amazon. Doc in any form other than their web-based existence.

Early methodologies for IT Planning in organizations viewed it as a response to a business strategy. However, it has become apparent that a more meaningful approach is to develop an integrated business and IT strategy. Such a strategy, for instance, may be designed through a careful analysis of all the marketing variables of the organization, namely product, price place and promotion, and by working out innovative IT based responses to issues such as differentiated products services to be offered; identifying and grooming market niche; linking with customers and suppliers; overcoming competition by building entry barriers and switching costs; and changing the balance of power in suppliers relationships. In other words, IT has become an inseparable ingredient of business strategy forming its core, rather than a supporting mechanism. One has to position IT in a proactive role, where the business strategy is not viewed as given, but one that can be challenged and reshaped in accordance with the potential available through IT.

The relationship between IT and Business Process Reengineering (BPR) has often been understated, perhaps due to a greater emphasis being given in the literature on the painful impacts of BPR. Concerned with radically redesigning the way work is done in organisations, BPR is almost totally driven by the capabilities of IT. The basic premise of BPR such as customer-driven processes, cross-functional teams, case approach, and delinearisation of work flow etc., can be realized only through the IT infrastructure behind it. It requires, of course, a change in the mindset, from looking at IT as a means of automating manual procedures to a resource for redesigning business processes.

Impact of IT Organisations — A Conceptual Framework

It is apparent from the above discussions that IT has an impact on organizations as a result of its capability to generate, process, disseminate and capture information, alter work flows and provide operational flexibility. This impact can be manifested in a variety of forms, some of which may be simultaneous, and some other may be mutually exclusive. Factors such as organization culture, management philosophy and economic and behavioural considerations in the organization influence the way these impacts take place The strategic vision of the top management has a key role to play in deciding the nature of IT applications and the ability of the organisation to derive strategic benefits from such applications.

Elaborating on these observations, a conceptual framework of the impact of IT on organisations has been developed by the authors through a rigorous process of research. The framework has the following key ingredients:

(a) The direct impact of IT on organizations is to provide timely and relevant information on key issues to those concerned, streamlining procedures, work flows and job designs, and providing operational flexibility.

(b) IT's ability to provide timely and relevant information

helps in enhancing intra-organisation and inter-organisation communication. These, in turn, facilitate improvement in the quality of decision making at various levels of management in the organization.

(c) IT's ability to streamline procedures, work flows and job designs, and to provide operational efficiency and flexibility, coupled with its ability inter- and intra-organisational communication, facilitate enhancement in the monitoring and control methods.

(d) Improvement in the quality of decision making at various levels, coupled with enhancement in monitoring and control methods, facilitate adoption of participative management, rationalising manpower and reducing the number of hierarchical levels in the organisation.

(e) The above structural changes facilitate either centralisation or decentralisation of decision making and creation of innovative forms for the organisation. These structural impacts, in turn, facilitate geographical expansion of the business of the organisation, enhance interactions with external agencies and promote synergy operations between various parts of organisation. Further, these help the organisation to enhance customer services and provide it a competitive advantage.

(f) The above impacts, put together, promote achievement of current organisational objectives, increase the ability of the organisation to adapt to its environment and help in increasing the match between organisational objectives and individual aspirations of employees. Thus, on the whole, these result in enhancing the overall organisational effectiveness.

This sequence of impacts can be further refined to develop a generic conceptual framework. The generic framework envisages three stages of the impacts of IT on organisations. In the first stage, IT influences various process variables. However, these first stage impacts are enabling in nature and it is not necessary that they would actually take place. If, however, they do take place, a range of options is thrown open for second stage impacts. These second stage impacts relate to structural variables; these may be in the nature of diverse impacts on organisation structure, such as reduction in the number of hierarchical levels, centralisation or decentralisation of decision making, and creation of innovative structural forms like the network organisation. In the third stage, the impact on structural variable is expected to be symbiotic with changes in process variables, i.e. the process changes will reinforce structural changes, and *vice versa*. The actual selection of the combination of various possible options will, however, be dependent upon the targets for organisational performance, such as enhancing customer service and gaining competitive advantage. The definition of these targets will be based upon a conscious need for enhancing the achievement of organisational effectiveness. Thus, eventually, organisational effectiveness may be enhanced as result of IT applications.

All the above mentioned impacts of IT do not take place automatically in any organisation, but require existence of certain favourable conditions or contingency factors. These can be defined as factors which exert a significant influence on the possible direction in which the impact of IT on the organisation may take place. Some of the key contingency factors are: top management style and commitment; organisational culture and value system; adequacy of financial resources, training of personnel, involvement of external change agents and meticulousness of planning. If the contingency factors act favourably, they will facilitate transformation of organisational processes and emergence of organisation structures, which promote achievement of the conceived performance variables. However, if they act in a counterproductive manner, IT may fail to have any significant impact on organisational effectiveness.

Empirical Findings

An empirical study carried out by the authors in an Indian organization engaged in providing software development services globally (hereinafter called IT Services Company), indicated that IT was perceived to have a high degree of impact on several process variables, namely providing timely information, providing operational flexibility and improving the quality of decision making at top management level. IT's impact on other process variables, namely providing relevant information, enhancing intra-organisational and external communication and improving the quality of decision making at the middle management level was perceived to be of a medium degree. Lastly, the impact of IT on streamlining procedures, improving the quality of decision making at the operating levels and enhancing the monitoring and control methods was perceived to be of a low degree. IT's impacts were perceived to be relatively less pronounced on structural variables, and it was predominantly seen to be promoting centralisation of decision making. IT's impacts on performance variables such as promoting geographical expansion, enhancing customer services and providing competitive advantage were perceived to be quite high.

The most important reasons for the success of IT in enhancing organisational effectiveness was perceived to be top management's commitment, meticulous training of personnel, adequacy of financial resources and conducive value system operating in the organisation. Besides, employee involvement and motivation, availability of requisite infrastructure for IT, and compulsions from the external environment were perceived to be important success factors. On the other hand, poor planning was considered as likely reason for not so successful impact of IT. Besides, inadequate concern in the organisation for improving internal systems and procedures, inadequate commitment towards systematic planning for IT, inadequate communication about available IT applications in the organisation, and lack of careful assessment of various alternative equipment and applications were perceived to be factor inhibiting the success of IT in enhancing organisational effectiveness. All these thus appear to be the major determinants of success of IT.

The empirical study did not derive any conclusive finding about IT and the centralisation/decentralisation debate. This is understandable on the ground that IT has the capability to provide information at all levels, but all such information may not find a role in decision making. It is difficult to categorically state that decision making invariably takes into consideration all the information and knowledge that is available in the organisation, irrespective of the level of authority. It is likely that the existing organisation culture and management philosophy may inhibit channelisation and use of information available at lower of hierarchy for decision making by the top management.

Pitfalls in IT-led Business Scenario

There is no doubt that IT has a pre-eminent place in the paraphernalia of management tools and techniques. However, it would be fallacious to consider it a panacea. Generating his expectations out of IT without understanding and appreciating its limitations can be disastrous. For instance, a myth surrounding IT has been that it would usher in the era of a paperless office. The capability of electronic storage of mass amount of data gives credence to this belief. Yet, the evidence is nowhere closer to it, and, ironically, the users of IT might have actually generated far more volume of paper than they have saved. This might be attributed to the mindset of a common user that paper-based information is more secure. That IT has resulted in information explosion is well known; but it may not be an exaggeration to say that this explosion has actually led to an information overload on the users, requiring disproportionately high efforts to separate the irrelevant from the relevant and sensible from the heap of not-so-meaningful information surrounding them. No wonder, decision makers at the end of it find it difficult to decide which information was relevant, and what else was there as garbage, though camouflaged as information.

IT has its own contributions to make in the human-created disasters. The Y2K crisis, fortunately, was averted, thanks to some of the toughest measures adopted by the IT industry years in advance of the impending crisis. It was one of the biggest challenges inadvertently created by human intelligence, but also effectively met by the same level of intelligence, though in the process, billions of dollars of money had to be spent. The point, however, remains that IT did contribute to a disaster in the making. The disaster caused by the ever-exploding computer-viruses are yet another phenomenon of major concern. The creation of new viruses and developing their antidotes have already taken the form of a flourishing industry. Hacking of websites, fraud and embezzlement through breach of network security and computer/internet based pornography are some other manifestations of how the capabilities of IT can be destructively engaged. The ethical issues arising out of the capabilities of IT to threaten the privacy of individuals can no longer be ignored, because in the internet driven IT applications, it is so much easier to track individual preferences, purchasing habits and lifestyles, and keep a watch on what an individual is doing on the web. Organisations, monitoring the e-mail transactions of their employees to prevent misuse of IT for personal gains, are perhaps justified in doing so, but they also give a glimpse into the potential to intrude into the private lives of individuals. The phenomenon of "Orwellian big brother", which didn't quite take place in 1984, as predicted by George Orwell has indeed arrived in the new millennium.

All this gloom talk is not to run down IT, but to have a fair perspective on the misuses which IT can be subjected to, and to keep the expectations from IT within realistic levels. It is also apparent that the onus for effective deployment of IT in organisations lies with the leadership provided by the top management. This, in turn, requires a long-term management vision and clarity of objectives.

Emerging Guidelines — The Mantras of Managing IT

For a practising manager to make optimal use of IT resources in his/her organisation, certain experiential guidelines can be provided. These are as follows:

(a) *Top Management Commitment*: While planning for introduction of IT in the organisations, total commitment and support from the top management should be sought. The role of top management would be crucial in deciding the dispersion of decision authority structure that would finally prevail in the organisation. This will also help in ensuring that due diligence is exercised while deciding about the requirement of the proposed IT applications and the approach to be followed for its induction.

(b) *Organisation Culture*: The strategy for introducing IT in the organisation should take into cognizance the existing organisation culture. At the same time, IT should be consciously and deliberately used to make the organisation culture more participation-oriented and conducive to strengthening the team-work and coordination between terms. Introduction of IT in an organisation is not a technological issue alone; it is also an important means of bringing about organisational transformation, in which culture and people are heed to have significant accompanying contribution, inseparable from that of IT. The top management should endeavour to transform the existing organisation culture so as to provide an internal environment supportive of the goals of enhancing organisational effectiveness through IT.

(c) *Meticulous Planning*: Introduction of IT applications should be carefully planned for. This would entail stating the objectives of IT applications by linking IT with the business objectives of the organisation, identifying the competitive advantages which IT can provide, and determining the specific IT application areas from the same. Planning for IT also includes a comprehensive documentation of the strategy and work plan for selection of hardware and software; design, development and testing of software, if custom-designed; installation and trial runs; training and final operation and maintenance of the IT system. Investment in IT should be need based and should be suitably budgeted for.

(d) *Preparing the Organisation for Change-Over*: Successful introduction of IT in the organisation requires preparing it for change-over, both operationally and in terms of mindset. Firstly, it should be ensured that suitable mechanisms for in-house dissemination of information on availability, expected benefits and guidelines for the Use of IT have been provided for and made use of in the organisation. This would also pave the way for active involvement of employees in the process. Training in all aspects of new systems and applications should be provided to the employees, so that they can competently work with the new systems without hassles, after and initial handholding. The process of introducing the new system should be timed in a manner that the conversion from the existing to the new system takes place with minimal disruptions. This may require parallel runs of the old and new system for some time, till the operating personnel gain confidence with new system. Alternatively, the strategy may be to introduce the new system in all parts of the organisation at an announced schedule in one go. Combinations of both these options may be possible depending upon specific needs of the organisation.

(e) *Involvement of External Change Agents*: A careful evaluation and selection of various aspects of IT is crucial to its successful application. Both over-engineered and under-engineered solutions are likely to yield-optimal results, despite the scale of investment made. Similarly, the process of introducing IT has all the ingredients of any process of change management, and need to be handled with sensitivity. For both these requirements, the involvement of external change agents is desirable. Two roles of external change agents can be envisaged; one as IT specialist would assist the organisation in making a judicious decision on the technological aspects, while the OD specialist will play a useful role in preparing the organisational personnel for changes being ushered in by IT.

Concluding Comments

The shape of IT has undergone incredible changes, and the accelerated pace of information generation ushered by it is unprecedented. This has resulted in much more dramatic intense impact of IT on organisational processes, structure, performance and effectiveness. The basic tenet of IT reflecting a convergence of computers of communications has not altered, and has in fact acquired bigger dimensions, and created global impacts. The interrelationship of IT and business strategy has become more pronounced, and IT appears to have permeated the core business of the organisation. In this process, however, some of the pitfalls of IT have become more glaring, necessitating a balanced approach. The conceptual model, reflecting the rationale through which IT can influence decision making, create structural impacts, enhance customer service, promote competitive advantage and increase overall organisational effectiveness, continues to be valid. Similarly, despite the nature of IT having changed, the need for a management approach to introducing and managing IT in the organisation remains as relevant today as was in the past.

Chapter 10

Establishing Self-Renewal Competencies

Change is the essence of life. Change takes place in organisations all the time. It may be induced by the pressures of the external environment or it may be the result of interpersonal dynamics within the organisation. It may be planned or may happen on its own. It may be occurring at a fast pace or may be slow-paced. It may be good for the organisation or may not be favourable. Yet, the fact is that one has to cope with the change. This coping with the change is not merely for individual members of the organisations, it is for the organisation as a whole. Further, it is not simply a one-time requirement but, a continuous process. It is therefore necessary that self-renewal competencies are established in organisation, so that they can develop internal capabilities for planning and managing change and can sustain these capabilities on a long-term basis.

This chapter presents some views on how self-renewal competencies can be established in organisations.

The Self-Renewal Process

Self-renewal is the process through which an organisation changes the configuration of its personnel while maintaining its identity. This implies that, in response to the need for adapting to the dynamics of the internal or external environment, the organisational personnel change their styles, attitudes, strategies, work methods and the like. In this process, it may be necessary to induct new people who have attributes in accordance with the newly desired responses. It may also be necessary to let some existing organisational personnel leave the scene, if their commitment to the desired values can't be built up owing to too deep an involvement with the values, which the organisation now wants to discard. However, all through this process, the organisation itself does not change its identity. And yet, it undergoes a great metamorphism; it has renewed itself and has ushered in new energy which can be effectively harnessed.

The self-renewal process may be reactive or proactive. It is reactive when the need for self-renewal is perceived in response to deteriorating organisational health, reduced effectiveness, low morale and other such adverse indicators. It may also be in response to sudden changes in the external environment; for instance, the Government may come out with new policies which, if made use of, can help the organisation prosper. Alternatively, the proactive mode of self-renewal may be the result of changes in the top management of organisation, when the new top management personnel have the desire to prove themselves, to leave their imprint on whatever happens to the organisation from now onwards. It may also be the result of an internal or external change agent, sincerely and meticulously planning for and bringing in change. In either case, there is always some key person in or outside the organisation, who senses the challenges and opportunities before the organisation and who makes all the strategic moves for self-renewal.

Creativity and Innovation for Self-Renewal

The self-renewal process does not take place in vacuum. It requires an application of creativity and innovation by a few key persons. Therefore, creativity and innovation are the two prime movers in the attainment of self-renewal capabilities by an organisation.

Creativity is "any thinking process that solves a given problem or achieves a given set of goals in an original and useful way." It is also the ability to see useful relationships about dissimilar things. It requires talent, originality and imagination. It also requires problem sensitivity, idea fluency, flexibility and drive. Some of the visible traits of creativity are ability to concentrate, reasoning power, communicative ability and skepticism.

Though certain individuals inherently possess creativity, it is also possible to acquire it through learning/training. Essentially, the learning of creativity involves learning to get rid of certain well known blocks to creativity. These may be perceptual block, cultural block, emotional block or mere habit. The perceptual block implies one's conditioning to a given frame of thinking in all situations. Removal of this block essentially requires frame breaking through conscious attempts. Cultural block refers to tendency to conform to the conventions and rituals of a given culture, with no attempt to outscope the same. Again, learning to remove this block requires conscious attempts. Emotional block is more mundane; it refers to psychological barriers such as fear of future, fear of ridicule etc.

Typically, the creativity process manifests itself into three phases. The first phase comprises familiarisation with the problem, involving orientation, data acquisition, examination and dissatisfaction with the existing solution. The second phase involves revelation, consisting of incubation, illumination and birth of new ideas. The final phase leads to development of the final solution, verification, control including periodic review and the satisfaction of having achieved something.

Innovation, on the other hand, is a new way of doing a thing. The emphasis here is on actual performance of tasks, albeit in a manner, which may be original, novel, more effective and leading to visible results.

Like creativity, innovative thinking or innovative practices may be inherent abilities of an individual or may be learnt. Learning or innovative abilities require a conducive organisational culture, and association of innovative applications with rewards and certain openness in the organisation towards risk taking.

Managing Change

Presumably, the applications of creativity and innovation lead to new strategies for the organisation. Implementation of these strategies involves change from the existing practices to newer, more effective practices. Once, the change has taken place and stabilised, the positive impact of the strategies will be felt. However, the immediate problem before an organisation is to introduce the change smoothly and totally.

Central to the issue of managing change are the processes of planning and implementing specific changes. These two processes are interdependent. The key requirement in this regard is to set the correct pace of bringing in change. If the pace is too slow, the whole endeavour of bringing in change may yield little results. On the other hand, if the process of change is very fast, it may be extremely difficult for most organisational personnel to adjust themselves to the required changes. The result may be a total failure of the planned strategies for change.

The process of change requires re-education for the organisation as a whole. The organisation must develop the capabilities to define the problem, generate hypotheses, and collect information from the total environment. It should also learn how to handle inadequate and conflicting data; how to trust feelings and attitudes, beliefs and facts; search for possible courses of action, viable alternatives and desirable solutions.

Levels of Change

Change has to be looked at from more than just a behavioural viewpoint because changes in behaviour are often a result of changes in knowledge and attitude. In fact, there are four levels of changes in people, namely knowledge changes, attitudinal changes, behavioural changes and group or organisational performance changes. Changes in knowledge tend to be easiest to make; all one has to do is to provide a person a book or article to read or have someone whom he respects, tell him something new. Attitude structures differ from knowledge structures in that they are emotionally changed in a positive or negative way. The addition of emotion often makes attitudes more difficult to change than knowledge.

Change in individual behaviour seem to be significantly more difficult and time consuming than either of the two previous levels. For example, a person may have knowledge about the potential dangers of smoking, even actually feel that smoking is a bad habit, he would like to change and still be unable to stop smoking because a habit pattern has been reinforced over a long period of time. It is important to point out that we are talking about change in patterned behaviour and not a single event. In our example, anyone can quit smoking for a short period of time; the real test comes months later to see if a new long-term pattern has evolved.

While individual behaviour is difficult enough to change, change of group of organisational performance is even more difficult. This difficulty is compounded, because at this level we are concerned with changing customs, mores and traditions. Being a group, it tends to be a self-reinforcing unit and therefore, a person's behaviour as a member of a group is more difficult to modify without first changing the group norms.

Recognising the Need to Change

The need to bring in change can be recognised by noticing one or more of the several signs of decay. These are observed, for instance, when behaviour of organisational personnel is oriented more to the past than the future; when there is a greater emphasis on the obligation of ritual than on the challenges of current problem; and when there is a greater allegiance to departmental goals than to company objectives as a whole.

The environmental pressures which necessitate these kinds of changes include the use of information technology which has narrowed decision time span, and mass communication system which have heightened public awareness of consumer products. Other important developments accelerating the need for organisational change are the dissemination of new management knowledge and techniques, globalisation of markets, increasing pressures for social equality and increase in Government demands and regulations.

The conceptual explanation of the need for change is based on two basic characteristics possessed by organisations. The first is the tendency to maintain and preserve a steady state. When one or more of an organisational elements are pulled out of balance there is a corresponding reaction on the part of organisation to mobilise its resources to maintain equilibrium. The second is the potential of the system to increase its internal capabilities and to expand its ability to influence the external environment. This is in fact, the potential for organisational growth and development.

Unfreezing, Change and Refreezing

It is widely recognised that change processes require unfreezing, changing and refreezing. No change process begins unless one recognises the need for change. Many processes help this process of unfreezing. These include the physical removal of the individual, from his accustomed routines, sources of information and social relationships, the suspension of all social supports, showing the consequences of continuing the way he is. On other occasions, it has helped to harness an opportunity provided by a humiliating experience or professional setback to cause change. Rewards and punishments have been known to cause unfreezing. In essence, unfreezing is the breaking down of the conditions and the mind-sets of the individual or the organisation.

After the unfreezing, the change process begins. The process of change requires identification of models and solutions from which learning can take place. Interactions occur when an individual is placed in a situation where new behaviour is demanded of him, if he is to operate successfully.

Yet the newly acquired behaviour can't be considered to have become 'permanent' until, it is integrated as a patterned behaviour into the individual's personality or an organisation's functioning. Once the new pattern is internalised after being learnt, refreezing is automatically facilitated, because it is fitted naturally into the personality of the individual and/or the organsiation.

Behaviour Modification

Behaviour modification as an approach to bring in change, is based upon observed behaviour. Also known as operant conditioning or reinforcement theory, behaviour modification's basic premise is that behaviour is controlled by its immediate consequences. Any behaviour will be made stronger or weaker by what happens immediately after it occurs. If what happens is positive, it tends to increase the frequency of that behaviour occurring again. Positive reinforcement is anything that is rewarding to the individual being reinforced. For instance, money might motivate some people to work harder; but to others the challenge of the job might be the most rewarding incentive. Managers must look for unique differences in their people and recognise the dangers of generalising. In order for a desirable behaviour to be obtained, the slightest positive behaviour exhibited by the individual in that direction must be rewarded as soon as possible. For example, when an individual's performance is low, one can't expect drastic changes overnight, regardless of changes in expectations or other incentives. Therefore, the manager must be aware of any progress of his subordinate, so that he is in a position to reinforce appropriately this change.

This is also compatible with the concept of setting interim rather than final goals and then reinforcing appropriate progress towards the final goals, as interim goals are accomplished.

While positive reinforcement tends to be more effective in working with people, experiencing some unpleasant consequences, negative reinforcement can sometimes strengthen a particular behaviour. A manager has to be careful in using negative reinforcement or punishment because he does not always know what he is reinforcing in a person, when he uses these methods. He might be reinforcing lying, manipulation of all kinds of undesirable behaviour, because the individuals involved may use these behaviours, rather than improved performance, to eliminate punishment or further negative reinforcement.

Another way to respond to behaviour, besides positive or negative reinforcement, is not to reinforce it at all. This is called extinction because it tends to get rid of a behaviour. People do not continue doing things that do not provide positive reinforcement.

Approaches to Management of Change

There are three possible approaches to bringing in organisational change. These are exercise of unilateral authority, sharing of power and lastly, delegated authority.

In the first approach, the change is implemented through authority derived from managers. The upper echelons of management define the problem, design the solutions and direct these downward through formal and impersonal control mechanisms. Actual method of execution may be by decree, replacement of key personnel or alteration of organisational structure.

In the second approach, there is an increasing emphasis to interactions and sharing of power. This may be achieved by group decision making, in which problem definition is by the top management and selection of one of the alternative solutions is done collectively. Alternatively, both the problem definition and solution may be done collectively, exposing organisational personnel to a wider decision making role and commitment. In the third approach, the complete responsibility for defining and acting on problems lies with the organisational personnel.

Empirical studies suggest that the second approach is usually the most successful.

Success of Change Management

It is observed that the successful cases of management of change are those which are spread throughout the organisation to include and affect many people; those which produce positive changes in the line and staff attitude; which prompt people to behave more effectively in problem solving and in relating to others; and those which observed that there is a greater probability of success in bringing about and managing change in cases where the organisation is under considerable external and internal pressure for improvement, long before an explicit organisation change is contemplated. Similarly, success has a better chance if the process of change is steered by a committed top management, perhaps a new team to the organisation having considerable personal stakes. In either case, the process of change involves collaborative efforts on the part of all levels. The top management provides catalytic support by providing others with new ideas and methods continually. The solutions and decisions are developed, tested and found credible on a small scale before an attempt is made to widen the scope of change to larger problems and the entire organisation. Lastly, the success of change has a cascading effect. The change effort spreads with each successful experience and as management support grows, is gradually absorbed permanently into the organisation's way of life.

It may be worthwhile here to distinguish between two types of change—the evolutionary and the revolutionary. The evolutionary change takes place on its own, as a result of dynamism within the organisation. Such a change is slow and its direction and thrust, is not easily influenced while the change is taking place. The revolutionary change, on the other hand, is a planned change which is brought about almost with a bang, requiring enormous effort on the part of organisational personnel to adopt it.

Change is a function of the dynamic balance of forces working in opposite directions, viz. driving forces and the restraining forces. This balance can be upset by adding to or increasing the driving forces or by removing or decreasing the restraining forces.

Bringing about a change is not easy. It requires overcoming inertia and ushering in movement in those components of the organisation which have been relatively inactive. It also requires a change in direction for some who are taking positions, contrary to the ones dictated by the new strategies. For some others, it requires an increase in pace though in the same direction.

An obvious assumption in the above thought is that change can be brought about only through people. In fact, the key variable in the organisation is its people must change. If change has to be brought about people must change first and in turn, should change other subsystems.

Concluding Comment

Organisation can be viewed as an organic system, which requires periodic self-renewal to survive and grow. Change is an inevitable phenomenon in any organisation. Creativity and innovation help in forecasting likely change and suggesting desirable improvements rather than being overtaken by force of events. Present-day managers should be able to implement planned changes smoothly if the organisation is to survive in the highly competitive environment.

This chapter dealt with the issues of self-renewal processes which is at the heart of organisational growth and renewal. Obviously self-renewal has to be rooted in one's own growth potential, competencies and traditions. Borrowed concepts alone make little headway unless organically rooted in the context and the real world. Accordingly, a brief look at the Indian ethos and illustrations reference to a couple of the corporate entities would facilitate appreciation of the concerns being voiced.

Charles Darwin's theory of survival of the fittest seems to be extremely relevant in the context of Indian organisations and hence the widespread concern and interest in organisational effectiveness. The concept of organisational effectiveness can be defined as the ability of the organisation to achieve pre-set goals and accomplish specified tasks from this statement, follows another inference of organisational effectiveness as the ability of the organisation to cope with the changing environment.

The organisations in the Indian environment must possess deep roots to withstand the turbulence created by its diversity. Accordingly, organisational structures which have emerged without adequate planning cast an effect upon the whole gamut of organisational processes. Before one delves into different organisational cultures and related aspects of cross-cultural influences, one must be clear on a shared understanding of Indian culture and its effects on managing people and processes.

The Indian Value Systems

Culture can be simply defined as an alternate mental construct of behaviour which influences organisational processes and hence, the organisational effectiveness. Indian cultural environment offers to its students a fascinating diversity in thought processes and behaviour, that it is embedded in a basic unity make the task of delineating and organisational culture manageable.

The Indian culture can be described as "collectivist" as compared to the "individualistic" culture that prevailed in the West. The peculiarity of the collectivist culture is a high degree of interdependence and preference for a tightly knit social framework. Individuals expect relatives/clients/others to look after them, in exchange for unquestioning loyalty. The relationship between the employee and his organisation is not a business relationship based on assurance of mutual advantages but has a moral component to it. Personal relationship considerations can take precedence over purely business considerations. People believe more strongly in the power of the individual than in the processes. Thus, the collectivist society has a social frame that is essentially individual centred rather than around the corporate whole. The whole fabric of social interactions in India are based on the personal relationship of 'trust' and if either of the two parties concerned detect a non-conformity to this principle, trouble appears.

The Indian value system and the Indian mind derives strength as well as infirmity from the Indian hierarchical system of family life. An individual suffers from power deprivation since early childhood. All decisions are taken by elders until a stage appears when the individuals almost lose confidence in their decision making capacity. The pent-up emotions of self-realisation of the "power factor" could be tackled in traditional organisation with the traditional frame of mind. But the problem gets compounded in a modern organisation composed of people from desperate cultures.

Similarly, it is easy to recognise that whereas any individual is primarily motivated by 'self interest' the Indian societal system makes 'self denial' as the ideal. Maintenance of harmony with others, in respect for age/authority, prestige and status consciousness, allergy to ambiguity, constant reference to the past are common manifestations of the Indian psyche.

The ancient Sanskrit texts of *Shukraneetee*, *Mudrarakshasa* and "Shantiparva" of *Mahabharata* shed light on Indian style of managerial functioning. Leadership qualities as delineated in Sanskrit texts resemble the qualities possessed by the father (encouraging), mother (forgiving), the teacher (building awareness), brother (democratic and fair), friend (loyalty), Kubera (God of Wealth) and Yama (God of Death). "Shantiparva" of *Mahabharata* emphasises on initiative and enterprise. The Indian manager needs to possess a nurturant behaviour, aiming to bring out the best in his subordinates.

Management is itself a symbolic activity. The manager influences other persons through wielding symbols that have meaning for these persons and motivate them towards desired actions. People are programmed differently by their different life experiences in different cultures. Hence, the management function of optimisation of resources for organisational effectiveness must take cultural reality into consideration.

Select Dimensions of Organisational Effectiveness: Case of Indian Public Sector Organisations

The criteria of organisational effectiveness are goal attainment (the end) and systems approach (the means needed to achieve the end) organisational performance is less than optimal due to process inefficiencies and approaches of the system members.

In this context, it is interesting to study Indian public sector organisations which are institutions founded with a viewpoint that was initially meant to provide impetus to the economy. Perhaps, two important concerns faced by the public sector organisations in India is the lack of role clarity between profitability and social obligations and lack of autonomy in operations.

A model relevant to public sector organisation has been developed in a United Nations Study in 1977, which suggests that organisational patterns and effectiveness is a function of its location, size, nature of technology and management environment. These factors are affected by task environment in the form of internal authority, public opinion, competition, supplies, trade union etc. This model recognising the constraints would be a measure of its effectiveness. Another study by the Foundation for Organisational Research (Delhi) on 192 managers listed the following factors for enhancing and hindering organisational effectiveness:

Factors Enhancing Organisational Effectiveness

—Export Leadership Team Spirit

Identification with organisational goals; Adoption of new systems: Systematic well-defined responsibilities.

Factors Hindering Organisation Effectiveness

Low identification of employees with organisational objectives: Poor systems and procedures: Union power; External constraints.

All the factors listed above have the inevitable common strain of cross-cultural influences on human relationship. To illustrate the above listed variable one can undertake a brief study, of four public sector organisation variables.

Case 1

Coal India Ltd. is a nationalised basic infrastructure industry having a workforce representing different socio-cultural backgrounds. Opinion survey among middle, management executives, revealed that CIL had considerable scope for improvement levels of organisation effectiveness. Suboptimal performance could be attributed in large measure to attempt for change structure without examining structure-strategy fit.

Organisational effectiveness has also been affected by the industrial relations situation. What is required is a proper fit between individual goals and organisational goals and better work attitudes all-round. Grievance handling mechanism needs to be made more sensitive and recruitment processes more scientific. It appears that technological upgradation was undertaken without taking into consideration, the people involved without sufficiently accounting for local conditions and infrastructure and support. There was insufficient feedback on implementation processes and no formalised arrangement for dissemination of information. The needed response to the above problems are obvious. But they cannot be worked out without the human endeavour to transcend cultural barriers and develop a commitment to the Coal India Ltd. culture.

Case 2

Power industry in general and BHEL in particular has been beset with low productivity and heavy losses. Power plant motor failures have been attributed to management failures and the inability of the task performers to sufficiently appreciate that quality has to be in-built into the system while designing the organisational structure. Sufficient provision should be made for communication between organisational groups participating in activities affecting quality since, quality is an interdisciplinary function. The total quality of the power plant system is the sum total of the individual quality of the works carried out by the individuals or groups. The need of the hour is to design tailor-made programmes designed for improving technical and human relation skills of the individuals and develop an organisational framework of reference to ensure that the system of data transmission functions properly.

Case 3

Steel Authority of India Ltd. figures in the list of top steel producing companies in the world. SAIL faces the problem of increase in manpower without increase in capacity. Experts suggest an overall reduction of 20 per cent in the workforce by the end of the century but continuity in recruitment is expected. SAIL faces low productivity and high labour costs, as a result of which its products are not competitive compared to U.K., Japan etc. The focus of HRD efforts have been on technical training (new entrants) and management development (executives). SAIL needs to further improve manpower planning based on the principle of rationalising and standardising. The training process needs to be organised with thought and knowledge of reinforcement. The concept of multi-job/multi-skill should be included in the training package to redo mental biases. Performance appraisal can be a powerful tool to correct cultural barriers if used properly. In the performance of planning and at reporting stage, the reporting officer can identify tasks to be accomplished that are based on self-appraisal and mutual discussions. This would help the appraisee to appreciate constraints, responsibilities and expectations of each other. After the subsequent stages of performance review and potential evaluation phase, job rotation plans and new jobs designs could be suggested. Manpower planning in SAIL needs to continually assess gaps in existing skills and desired levels and needs to review work methods and practices from time to time.

Case 4

E.I.L. operates in a complex dynamic environment with a great degree of uncertainty in decision making. It uses matrix organisations which gives total responsibility to the project manager to plan, co-ordinate and integrate functional requirements. The trouble spots in the system are accountability factor and the short-lived nature of project teams. A project involving task force from diverse functional specialisation necessitates adoption of team approach to achieve a common objective. The project and functional personnel require improvement in their responsibility-authority relationships with increased urgency of trust and team spirit.

The Remedy

The reasons cited for hindered organisational effectiveness are varied as suggested by the foregoing illustration. But, perhaps the most important of them is the lack of a consistent culture. Dr. N.C.B. Nath, Chairman, Foundation Aid Industrial Recovery remarks—"To my mind the public sector has three strains of culture—the culture of business, the culture of administration and the culture of politics. My hypothesis is that the Indian public sector is value neutral."

> "Given a certain kind of leadership it will talk of business, given another kind of leadership, it will talk the language of political manipulation, of propriety, if the Indian public sector has one consistent language, I see no reason why we will not have effective organisation."

Organisational effectiveness can be enhanced using the quality circle concept. The primary strategy for deploying Quality Circle concept is a conducive organisational climate and work culture. Quality Circle members should also be given autonomy in decision making.

The process quality model lists critical success factors as:

— Leadership

— Excellent customer satisfaction: Adaptation to change and exploitation of new technology and business opportunity.

Team building is another simple way of disentangling the different barriers created by cross-cultural influences. Studies conducted by Mayo show that the amount of work done by a worker is equivalent to his social capacity and not his physical capacity. Hawthorne studies further show that workers react as members of a group and the level of production are set by social norms and not by psychological capacities. Team building as a method of change can be viewed as a system having input variable, process variable and output variable. The input variable would be background factors, attitudes like personality attributes and values. Process variables are internal influences like style of leadership, language, interaction, behaviour, decision style employed by the team. The output variables are results of team interaction like team spirit, information sharing etc. The group liabilities are social pressure, individual domination, balance of solution (skilled manipulator leads) conflicting secondary goals winning the argument.

Teams need to possess an internal mechanism for conflict resolution. Conflict is caused by competition, domination and provocation. Disagreements between clashing parties can be resolved by the following methods:

— All parties concerned should come together.
— Agree that there is a problem and have responsibility to work it out.
— Team building is, not to like each other but to understand each other and to be able to work together.

Leadership is another critical factor affecting organisational performance. The style of leadership and his/her qualities permeates the whole organisation and affects its functioning. Leadership style should be flexible and should suit the situation. It should also develop a commitment for nurturance of the personnel that comes under their wing. "Culture is caring for the young who are in your charge." I think this is what makes for organisational excellence.

Appropriate Indian managerial techniques of *Sama* (persuasion), *Dama* (rewards), *Danda* (punishment) and *Bheda* (discrimination) could be used to lead and resolve conflict. Human nature according to Indian tenets are of three varieties—*Sattva*, *Rajas* and *Tamas*. The 'Sattva' person is knowledge oriented and responds better to consulting and participation process. The 'Rajas' person is action oriented and requires supervision and guidance at crucial points of operation. The 'Tamas' person is good at physical work and needs to be monitored at each step. The manager must use the technique appropriate to the dominant *guna* in the individual, at that particular situation.

The team-building process for reordering the organisation would develop interpersonal relations by unfreezing, change and refreezing. Team building and other appropriate training programmes unite people into a cohesive group to build a synergistic organisation resulting in a high level of performance. It is also important that people in power support changes.

Cross-cultural influences need not essentially have a baneful effect on organisational effectiveness. Instead cross-cultural influences can be used to enhance performance with the help of team-building, greater organisational communication between work groups and organisational reinforcement techniques for development of a unique organisational culture which promotes commitment to the company objectives. This has to be accounted for while looking at strengthening and establishing self-renewal competencies of organisations.

Chapter 11

Organisation Development System: The Emerging Concerns

So far, the effort has been to explain the organisation development process and elaborate upon some of the key concerns, methods and techniques. That organisations are organismic has been elaborated upon. Since, they are organismic, they are bound to change. Organisation development provides a conscious planned effort to give shape, pace and direction to this change. The approach to organisation development has believed in a closed loop relationship amongst the variables of the organisation. Once it is recognised that there is a situation needing attention, the approach involves isolating the symptoms and identifying the causes, structuring of the causes, unfreezing, intervening and refreezing; and then going back to the analysis of the prevailing situation. This approach is both time tested and effective. Organisation development, however, has to keep pace with the changing environment and changing times, no less than changing technologies.

Emergence of Information Driven Organisations

The borderless world is open to the power of technology penetration and traditional boundaries of disciplines give way to concerns of effectiveness and efficiency. The art of survival also seems to require the expertise of the science of survival. In such a flux, the various concerns of organisations need to be understood afresh, perhaps redefined. Some conventional definitions bear scrutiny; others seem to be dying a slow death. The air is ripe with controversies and this modest effort clearly lays no claims at resolving them. By the nature of this effort, there is a professional compulsion to indicate some of the emerging issues so that leads can be provided for the future.

Clearly, organisations now have moved from an era of being finance driven and subsequently technology driven to an era, where they are information driven. Information as a resource is nothing new to the running of the organisation or to the process of decision making. Many may rightly consider it to be the very heart of decision making process. What is new, however, is programmed mechanical competencies of data processing analysis and, what should not be forgotten, data synthesis. The earliest data processing equipment to be provided in India was in the early seventies. Since then, the two decades plus of experience has shown the permeation of computers in several organisations. The most important features of the adoption of computers are now possible to discern. Typically, Indian organisations have seen a rapid dissemination of decision support systems, specifically spreadsheets. This is to be recognised and applauded even though the number of organisations covered such penetration need to grow many more times. Of course, one does not, by implication, take the position that all organisations irrespective of their size and focus need to utilise computer technology instantaneously. What is clear, however, is that there is an area of organisational functioning, which leads one to be hopeful, not only about the growth of Indian organisations, but also indeed the information technology industry in India being truly global and competitive.

Information Technology: Newer Configurations

It is impossible to count and trace the almost endless applications of information technology in organisations. In fact, there can be as many applications of information technology, as can be the strands of creativity in the human mind. If the information technology, broadly defined to include data collection, storage processing and retrieval to the fourth or fifth generation computers and advanced communication technologies, is the driving force of organisation management, then evidently, the organisation structures, processes, job designs, organisation design and indeed the very act of decision making cannot be left untouched.

Expert systems have emerged in the recent past, widening the frontiers of information technology from data processing to knowledge engineering. The implications for organisations are interesting; they seem to be looking for personnel possessing skills in areas hitherto not searched for. They now look for a knowledge engineer, who can pick up knowledge from experts and place it into the computer based system; a programmer, who understands social sciences; a systems analyst, who understands the issues related to management of change. A whole new species of organisation persons is about to break the cocoon and emerge into the world of organisations. The trainer, has started wondering why the traditional training programmes on project management, leadership, attitude building etc. are no longer favourites of the sponsors. In his role as a developer, he is beginning to recognise that the organisation world of the future will belong to the half breeds. A mechanical engineer with the appreciation of electronics, takes hold of the manufacturing processes and individuals with social sciences background attempt to combine in themselves the strength of engineering methods to keep their understanding of the organisational processes clear. The types of combinations can be endlessly listed.

As organisation structures get integrated, the flow of information is likely to determine the shape of organisations. The organisation person had been talking of vertical integration of data processing, now he is concerned with lateral integration. All this has raised the value of human input into organisation management, where strategic decisions have become more critical to organisation survival than ever before. This has induced, for instance, emergence of product based organisation structures, as compared to division based organisation structures.

It is no longer easy to create additional tiers of organisation structure to accommodate vagaries of the personnel systems of the organisations. There is a pressure on organisations to reduce the response time and answers are being sought in reducing the numbers of hierarchical levels in the organisation from the coveted 11 or 9 to 5 or less. Modular form of organisation structures, like flexible manufacturing systems, seems to hold the key to the future. Networking and specialisation or one aspect of production or servicing seem to be the force of some global giants. The air is also thick of the talk of robotics, computer aided manufacture, process control instrumentation and computer aided design.

Further enhancements in the use of advanced communication technologies such as electronic mail, teleconferencing, electronic money transfer systems and the like are expected to permeate Indian organisations sooner than later.

View on the Impact of Information Technology

Obviously, the impact of information technology on organisations is profound though there have been differing views, predictions and empirical evidence regarding this impact. One view has been that there will be virtual elimination of middle management position in organisations since most of the strategic decisions can be taken by the top management with the use of information technology by directly processing information obtained from operating levels. A diametrically opposite view has been that there will be an enhancement in the role of middle management, since persons holding such positions in organisations will be able to sit back and think big for a change, having delegated many of their routine functions to information technology. Another view is that information technology will have little influence on organisation structures while yet another view is that the impact of information technology on organisations will in reality depend upon the management philosophy governing the introduction of information technology in the organisations.

Several perspectives appear in literature for viewing the impact of information technology on organisations. One of these is 'Technological Determinism', which implies that technical forces are the decisive factors in generating socio-economic change. In other words, decisions are made on the basis of technological capabilities rather than on the basis of human needs. However, this perspective has been debated on the ground that technology is not neutral, the development of a technology is the consequence of perceived gain of dominant interest groups of businessmen, who invest R&D efforts and finances in such preferred areas.

Another perspective for viewing impact of IT on organisations is that of "segmented institutionalism" which implies that organisations are inherently political in nature and information technology provides set of tools for acquiring and exercising powerful position through manipulation of the political processes of the organisation. The opposite perspective is that of "systems rationalism", as per which organisations are indeed rational systems and information technology helps performance of rational organisational processes more effectively.

It is obvious that the various perspectives mentioned above have relevance in specific contexts but none of them can be deemed to be universal truth. The ability of the top management of an organisation lies in promoting these value systems amongst organisational members, which are in tune with the systems rationalism perspective. Within such perspective, the specific changes, which may result in the organisation structures and processes of the organisation in focus, would then depend upon the nature and shape of information technology, the objectives for which it was introduced and the process of introducing information technology.

The empirical evidence indicates that there are enormous variations in the experience with and outcomes of introducing IT in organisations. A number of factors appear to influence the actual impact which IT may have in specific cases. These factors include, for instance, the extent to which those who work in the organisation share its goals and values, approach chosen for the introduction of technology, top management philosophy, economic factors, Government regulations etc.

Another significant factor to be considered in this regard is that information technology is not monolithic, it comprises multiple technologies, each of which may differ from the other in terms of the nature and degree of impact, which may in many instances be in different directions.

The contingency view is also supported by an economic perspective on the impact of IT. As per the perspective, IT promotes both centralised and decentralised decision making. On one hand by improving the quality and speed of information processing, it promotes centralisation; on the other hand, through improved monitoring capabilities and performance evaluation schemes, it promotes decentralisation. Similarly, by providing the management with an ability to manage a large organisation effectively, IT induces an increase in organisational size. However, on the other hand, IT also induces reduction in organisational size by providing cost-effective means to operate in a market kind organisational environment and thus promoting market operators. Thus, IT appears to have two opposing effects on organisations, whose net effect may vary from situation to situation.

An innovative implication of the introduction of IT in organisation is the emergence of networked organisations. These networked organisations comprise organisational personnel along with their shadow IT partners which provide them unprecedented power to access, process, store and communicate knowledge and which enable a knowledge worker to be in contact with other knowledge workers. This helps creation of a market like structure inside an organisation, which is superimposed over the traditional hierarchical structure and is characterised by rich electronic communications, permeable boundaries, flat structure, inter-dependent responsibilities, organic form and extended integration through strategic alliances.

Another manifestation of IT's impact on organisations is observed in the emergence of team based problem focused, often changing work groups, supported by electronic communication. Thus, IT can be seen to be promoting group decision making.

Yet another view emerging in the recent years is that IT essentially provides a new approach to effectively managing interdependence. This means increased ability of an organisation to achieve concurrence of effort along multiple dimensions of the organisation, and is achieved as a result of vastly improved communication capabilities, helping in wiring together of individuals and suborganisations within a firm and amongst firms.

Developing Theory of the Impact of IT on Organisation

The authors have carried out selective investigations in a few organisations to build up a theory of the impact of information technology on organisation, structures and processes. Some of the key features of this emerging theory are as follows:

(a) The direct impact of information technology in most organisations is perceived to be providing timely and relevant information to all organisational personnel, enhancing intra-organisation communication and external communication, streamlining procedures, work flows and job designs and providing operational efficiency and flexibility.

(b) These direct impacts result into the benefits of improving the quality of decision making at top management and operating levels, enhancing monitoring and control methods, promoting participative management and rationalising the manpower strength of organisation concerned.

(c) A further consequence of these impacts on organisations is observed in terms of reducing the number of hierarchical levels in organisations, promoting autonomy, on one hand, or promoting centralisation, on other hand, depending upon the value system within the organisation, promoting geographical expansion of organisational functioning and enhancing interactions with external agencies.

(d) These trends/changes in organisations facilitate emergence of innovative organisation structures. These structures may take the form of flat organisations, networked organisations, symphony organisations/ market form the unique characteristics and environment of a specific organisation.

(e) Whatever innovative form the emergent organisation structure may take, it is expected to lead to the key benefits of enhancing customer service, providing strategic advantage/competitive edge and enhancing the management of interdependence in the organisation.

(f) The above benefits will promote achievement of current organisational objectives, environmental adaptability of organisations and compatibility with personal objectives of organisational personnel. Thus, on the whole, these result in enhancing the overall organisational effectiveness.

The impact of information technology on organisations, as we observe today, is merely a tip of the iceberg. Lot more revolutionary possibilities exist for information technology to reorient itself and consequently influence the organisation structures and processes. Many of these possibilities may be visible today in a broad outline form; however, many more may still be in a pre-conceptualisation stage. All one can say at present is that the future organisations may have virtually no resemblance to the present day organisations. How different they will be, only future will tell.

While Winding up the Book: A case is presented on the Impact of Information Technology on Organisation Structure and Processes.

The revolutionary changes taking place in information technology (IT) and its applications have significant implications for effective functioning of organisations. While, on the one hand, IT is creating a new information society characterised by accelerated change, globalisation and increasing complexity, on the other hand, IT is also enhancing the ability of the organisations to deal effectively with these very characteristics of the information society. The organisations engaged in providing IT related services, such as designing IT strategies, information systems planning, application software development etc. are expected to be fully aware of the potential of IT in enhancing organisational effectiveness of their client organisations. How much do they themselves make use of the strengths of IT and how much they themselves have benefited from IT, have always been issues of inquisitiveness. One of the authors had the opportunity to observe from close quarters the applications of IT in a prominent IT services company in India and the impacts of these IT applications on its own organisational effectiveness. This case outlines the findings of the author on these issues in the context of this particular company.

About the Company

The company in question (hereinafter called the IT company) is a large, export oriented organisation providing IT services in diverse sectors such as banking and financial services, manufacturing industries, energy, health care, transport, communications and tourism. The IT company strives hard to stay at the forefront of technology and uses its innovations for providing solutions to clients' problems. The services offered by the IT company include hardware sizing and capacity planning, development of application and systems software, communications and networking, software project management, implementation and training. It conducts feasibility studies and assists its clients to scientifically plan their information systems, including the identification of the appropriate technology and design requirements. It is continually developing world-wide custom built software involving large data bases, computer aided design, office automation and local and wide area networking. Besides, it also markets and supports several off-the-shelf software products.

The IT company has offices in all major cities in India, as well as, in important cities in USA, Europe, the Middle East and the Asia Pacific Region. A considerable part of its own investment in IT is therefore devoted to providing communication facilities amongst these offices. Some of the communication technologies in which the company has invested include telephones, hotlines, telex, facsimile equipment and electronic mail. In addition, it has set up dedicated data communication links and video-conferencing facilities with select client organisations in USA, Canada and Europe. Other investments in IT by the company include mainframe computer systems for data processing of client transaction and for off-site software development. Similarly, it has invested in mini-computer systems of several kinds, which are used as 'target' machines for software development work. Several localised software solutions have also been developed by the company to support important functional areas such as cost control, manpower allocation, financial accounting, payrolls, personnel data bases etc. The company has provided dedicated hardware resources to most of its professionals in all offices, enabling them to depend more on technology than on manpower for carrying out their professional work. The company has, in fact, consciously built up a work culture which values self-help and which discourages the proliferation of clerical and class four staff in the organisation.

Perceptual Survey

In order to assess the impact of IT on the organisation structure and processes in the IT company, the authors launched an empirical research. A part of this empirical research was the conduct of a perceptual survey with a select sample of 84 respondents from the company. These respondents represented various branches of the company in different geographical locations, various functional areas and various levels in the organisation's hierarchy. While selecting the respondents, care was taken to ensure that the respondents had been a part of the company for a considerable period, so as to have adequate familiarity with the applications of IT, as well as, with the organisational culture in the IT company.

The questionnaire for the perceptual survey comprised five parts. The first part dealt with the impact of IT on the processes and structural variables of the IT company. The second part was related to the impact of IT on the overall organisational effectiveness of the company. Parts III and IV were concerned with identifying the reasons for success and relative failure, if any, respectively, of IT in enhancing organisational effectiveness of the company. Lastly, Part V pertained to the likely future scenario of introduction of IT in the company and its likely impacts.

The respondents had to give their responses on an ordinal scale of 1 to 5 for Part I of the questionnaire. The ratings on the ordinal scale comprised 1 (virtually no impact), 2 (impact to some extent), 3 (fair degree of impact), 4 (substantial impact) and 5 (very high degree of impact). The Part II also had an ordinal scale of 1 to 7, comprising disastrous impact, negative impact, no impact, marginal positive impact, fair degree of positive impact, substantial positive impact and an exceptionally high positive impact. Parts III and IV had listed predetermined multiple responses and the respondents could tick one or more of these responses. Part V was, however, totally unstructured.

Based on an analysis of the responses, weighted average values were computed for Parts I and II; these were interpreted as degrees of impact corresponding to the nearest values on the ordinal scale. In the case of Parts III and IV, percentages of total responses were computed for each possible factor and the key reasons for success and 'relative failure' of IT were identified. These findings have been summarised in the next section.

Impact on Organisational Processes and Structural Variables

The survey indicated that most of the respondents perceived a fair degree of impact of IT on organisational processes such as provision of relevant and timely information to all concerned, quality of decision making at top, middle and operating levels of the organisation, enhancing the capabilities of intra-organisational communications and communications with external organisations. A fair degree of impact was also observed towards increasing operational flexibility in the organisation. However, interestingly, the impact of IT was perceived to be only to some extent in enhancing the monitoring and control methods in the organisation.

Some other interesting perceptions were obtained regarding the impact of IT on structural variables of the IT company. It was generally perceived by the respondents that IT promoted participative management in the organisation only to some extent. On the other hand, IT appeared to have a fair degree of impact in promoting centralisation in the organisation, while it did not appear to promote decentralisation. It was also felt that by most respondents IT did not significantly lead to creation of innovative organisational forms/structure, nor did it significantly lead to reduction in the number of hierarchical levels in the organisation. Similarly, it was generally perceived that IT resulted, only to some extent, in streamlining of procedures, work flows and job designs and rationalising of manpower strength in the organisation. It may be worthwhile mentioning in this context that the IT company has a matrix organisation structure in operation, characterised by creation of multi-disciplinary project teams which are reconfigured with the commencement of new projects, based on the nature of skills demanded in each project.

Impact on Performance Variables and Organisational Effectiveness

Substantial impact of IT was perceived by the respondents towards some of the performance variables of the organisation. For instance, it was generally felt that IT has substantially helped in promoting geographical expansion of the organisation enhancing quality of customer services and in providing a competitive advantage to the organisation. It was also perceived that there is a fair degree of impact of IT in terms of increased sharing of information and interactions with external organisations and also an increased synergy of operation between various parts of the organisation.

Judging the impact of IT on the three dimensions of organisational effectiveness made interesting observations. IT was perceived to contribute a fair degree in achieving the current organisational objectives of the IT Company. IT was also perceived to have a fair degree of impact in enabling the IT company to adapt to its environment. However, its impact in terms of promoting a match between individuals' objectives and the objectives of the organisation was perceived to be only to some extent. On the whole, a fair degree of impact of IT was perceived in enhancing the overall organisational effectiveness of the IT company.

Key Reasons for Success and Relative Failure

The response indicated that top management commitment towards effective use of IT was perceived to be the most important reason for the fair degree of success of IT in achieving organisational effectiveness. Other important reasons were perceived to be training of personnel, adequate financial investments by the company in IT and its conducive organisational value system and culture.

On the other hand, key reasons for relative failure of IT in making a substantial or a very high degree of impact were perceived to be poor planning, top management style, inadequate training and inadequate involvement of external change agents. It was interesting to observe that while a section of respondents attributed the success of IT to adequate training, a small cross-section attributed 'relative failure' of IT to inadequate training. Similarly, while, poor planning was considered as the most important reason for relative failure of IT, meticulous planning was perceived as an important reason of success of IT in enhancing organisational effectiveness by a section of the respondents.

Future Scenario of IT

It will also be of interest to share the expectation of the respondents regarding future scenario of IT in the IT company. A widely shared perception of the respondents was the need to have enterprise wide networking with centralised data bases and networking with clients and external data sources. The need to have a dedicated and interconnected PC at every table to act as a nodal point for information retrieval and communication was also emphasised by the respondents. It was visualised by them that technological innovations of this kind will help the company enhance its operational flexibility, promote increased interactions with external organisation, as well as, enhance intra-organisation communications. It was also felt that these effects will further result in increased and quick availability of information and thereby improve the timeliness and quality of decision making. It was also perceived by some respondents that this will help the company enter new areas of business and promote geographical expansion of its operations. However, interestingly, it was widely perceived that centralisation will continue to be the governing philosophy of the company despite (or perhaps because of) IT and its potential.

Conclusions

The findings of the perceptual survey seem to indicate that the first level effects of IT are on organisational processes such as information flow, internal and external communication, decision making, operational flexibility and monitoring and control. These effects are enabling in nature; however, it is not necessary that these effects should actually take place. For instance, in the present case, the effect on monitoring the control systems has been only to some extent.

The second level effects of IT appear to be on the organisation's structural variables such as centralisation, decentralisation, number of hierarchical levels, streamlining of procedures, work flow and job designs and rationalising manpower strength in the organisation. Alternatives for structural changes appear to emerge as a result of process changes, occurring due to the impact of IT. In the present case for instance, the trend towards centralisation appears to be more pronounced than towards other types of structural changes. This also appears to be influenced by contingency factors, such as, organisation's culture and value system, method of introducing IT in the organisation and managing IT related change.

The third level impact of IT appears to be on the performance variables such as geographical expansion, customer services, competitive advantage etc., and through them to the three dimensions of organisational effectiveness. This impact appears to be perpetuated through a mutually reinforcing relationship between changes in structural and performance variables. In the present case, there appears to be a substantial degree of third level impact.

Thus, this illustrative case study validates the theory of the impact of IT on organisational structure and processes and organisational effectiveness, propounded by the authors.

To Conclude

This chapter was the last, but not the least. It brought out the emerging concerns relating to organisation management. It dwelt at length into the emergence of information driven organisations and the newer configurations brought about by information technology. It narrated some of the well known views on the impact of information technology on organisations and evolved a theory outlining the various stages of this impact.

How valid is this theory in practice? An attempt has been made by the authors to answer this question in the following case study. The name of the organisation has been withheld to conceal its identity. However, enough information is available to appreciate the issues involved and specific situational factors, which may have led to the impacts, as they have been observed and recorded in the case.

The readers will do well to carry out an empirical research to substantiate or modify the theory presented here. This does not necessarily require conducting a perceptual survey, as has been done in this case. You may interview key persons in an organisation where you are aware of the impact of information technology and ascertain as to how exactly information technology is influencing the organisation.

You may also like to read about the changes taking place in the organisations in countries such as USA, Canada, and Japan. There are several sources for such information; your library is surely full of current journals which will provide enough examples. Just document these examples carefully, analyse the information compiled and you will have enough material at hand to provide the glimpses of the emerging organisations in your own country.

A book such as one you have been reading cannot conclude. It is a continuing experience in your life and in understanding of organisations and organisation development process. It is hoped that as you evolve and grow further some of the ideas you may have picked up in the book shall get mellowed and perfected still more to help you to reach greater and more insightful meaning into your experiences.

Chapter 12

Organisation Development Systems: The Emerging Concerns-II

Emergence of Global Organisations

In the last decade or so, changes in design, context and forms of organizations have not only been substantial, but also radical. Not that the old form has ceased to exist, but only that the organizational genealogy has evolved to a higher level of evolution.

This Chapter not only seeks to cover some of the global trends in organizational forms of last six years but also shows how future has become present in many parts of the world. This concurrency of the past forms with what was thought of as on-line existence with the future firms already operative provides a kaleidoscope in time.

The Organization Management specialists, while recognizing this reality, have yet to bring it to the level of classroom situations and learning events in a structured manner. The attempt to outline the trend therefore marks an effort not only to show where we are but includes what could be a growing pattern of organization design.

While the pyramidical, the pentagonal, the allegial, the mixed matrix and other forms of organization will continue to be real, what matters today is the organizational form of knowledge systems walking across the field as virtual organizations. The Multinational Corporations with backward and forward linkages from pre-mechanized era to the mechanized one are simultaneously operating in automated environments. The kind of demands this kind of situation can make on organizational processes, work designs and decision models have to be comprehended to be able to face the future better.

Raw material coming from one type of social milieu, being fabricated and converted into internal components in a different milieu, to be assembled in a third, and to be marketed in a fourth era of time, is no longer a rare phenomenon. This scenario has become typical of global organizations today like never before.

Challenges Facing Global Organisations

A global organization does not survive without undergoing its own share of shocks and tribulations, which impact not only the people within, but also the entire gamut of HRD processes related to the organization. The global organization has to be concerned with global strategies which demand global integration of its operations, whether related to production or marketing or supply chain or even finance. At the same time, a global organization can overlook the demands for local responsiveness at its own perils. A global strategy without local responsiveness will fall short in implementation and will fail to deliver at the level of interface with the local environment, which demands quick decision making and flexibility of approach according to the situation at hand. Very often immediate actions have to be taken at the local level keeping into consideration the local sensitivities and often without having the benefit of an overarching global strategy to guide. Though information technology does provide the necessary resources in the form of feedback on local challenges and policy guidelines which can be fed to the local levels fairly quickly, it is often not possible to guarantee that such a global strategy has fully captured the subtle nuances of cultural or people-related complexities. Thus is where a global organization confronts its first challenge.

Despite this inherent barrier of the imperative to deal responsively with local situations, the importance of a unified global strategy can't be overemphasized for a global organization. The global organization stands for a unique identity, a unique value system and a unique brand image, which has to be carefully nurtured. This derives itself, not only from the economic imperatives of the international situation in which the global organization is functioning, but also from an HRD perspective. The people in the organization whether stationed in India or Japan or Europe or anywhere else would identify themselves with that singular identity. The economic context of the global organization of course dictates the policy level parameters, which require blending with the HRD-driven demands for identity. Thus, overall, the global organization strives for a certain level of global integration of culture and value systems and effective co-ordination to ensure that this happens across various parts of the organization, spread apart geographically and culturally.

The various geographically- and culturally-spread parts of the global organization pose an additional challenge towards organizational learning. It is necessary to encourage free flow of information, knowledge and wisdom from one part of the organization to another so that creativity is not stifled, and overall the organization gains from such exchanges. At the same time, this organizational learning process has to be professionalized and streamlined so that the exchange of information, knowledge and wisdom is documented or digitized, and is allowed to traverse through a properly designed information technology infrastructure. While such professional processes can be expected to take care of the flow of explicit knowledge, the need for regular exchange of tacit knowledge can't be lost sight of. This exchange requires for periodic international face-to-face meetings, global events or deputations from one part of the organization to another in order to allow enough opportunity for intermingling and learning from each other through contact.

Developing Global Mindset

Perhaps the most difficult challenge for a global organization is to develop the attributes of a global mindset in all sections of its employees located in different parts of the world. This is easier said than done. The thinking pattern of typical human resources is usually so much engrained in the local milieu that such a transformation is difficult to achieve without a systematic coaching process. To be true, no one is born with a global mindset. It is a trait which has to be learnt and refined through practice. The demand for having global mindset is obviously higher for higher echelons of management, and to be fair, even the opportunities available for this transformation are also higher for them. Yet, even at lower echelons, which are at the interface with local conditions, the demand for global mindset exists and the barriers to this are also higher.

This poses several questions to the top/corporate level HRD personnel in the global organization. A fundamental question is whether it is indeed desirable and feasible to make every manager fully endowed with global mindset qualities (and how to measure the degree of such an endowment). The related question is that of financial investments (and that of other resources) required for this ambitious goal. The issue is also related to the classical issue of lateral entry *vis-à-vis* in-house grooming of persons with global mindset qualities. Last but not least, the question to be carefully considered by the global organization is the degree of emphasis it should place on the potential of managers to become global in their attitude in the entire selection process. The answer to these questions may lie in the nature of business in which the organization is engaged.

There is no doubt that information technology has become a key driver of the ever-increasing trend towards evolution of the global mindset. The opportunities, of continual interpersonal communication and communication with vendors and customers, geographically separated through channels such as e-mail and messaging, facilitate dispersion of ideas and fusion of local mindsets into something more global and eventually identified as the global mindset of the organization as a whole.

Global Organisations: The Diversity Challenge

A global organization typically comprises a diverse workforce. This diversity is reflected in nationalities, cultures, religions and traditions. The diversity is manifested in various manners such as the language for communication, work culture, management style, attitude towards hierarchy, approach to teamwork, way of expressing agreement and disagreement, participation in decision making and communication styles etc. This diversity is important not only from the point of being politically correct but also because it can become a source of competitive advantage to the global organization. At the level of each local interface in the same or in a different country, the global organization presents a local face to the local milieu comprising the society, government, social subsystems and of course the local customers. This is important because it facilitates developing and maintaining affinity with the local culture, which is essential for its survival in the local context. Speaking the local language, understanding local traditions and rules of behaviour, respecting local values and even believing in local superstitions become important attributes for integrating effectively with the society leaders, government officials, local vendors and customers and several other local stakeholders. This also provides certain internal advantages such as improved ability to attract and retain local talent and improved knowledge sharing.

Obviously diversity is important for a global organization and it takes active measures to promote and nurture diversity. However, while doing so, the global organization has to keep in focus the need for a certain common trait that runs across all fragments of the organization, and which are key to its global survival. For example, a global organization would require that there should be common norms of interaction (shared decision making and teamwork), organization-wide communication language, and commonly shared qualities of conduct and elements of behaviour. This also includes, though not necessarily explicitly stated, subscription to basic values of trust and integrity weaving throughout the spread of the global organization. This may appear paradoxical to the characteristics of diversity just mentioned above, but is not so. The global organization requires this dual approach due to its inherent structure. What is necessary is that these apparently opposite requirements are effectively balanced all the time, and they actually complement each other.

Organizational Learning in a Global Organization

While the importance of continual organizational learning in a global organization can't be overemphasized, it is also true that owing to its very complexity, the global organization faces a variety of impediments in this process. Difficulties arise when the strategic value systems of the organization are not shared effectively organization-wide, which would have been the theme around which the learning processes in the organization may be focused. This might happen when short-term thinking pervades and longer term investment in knowledge accumulation is not considered critical. The obvious remedy is that sharing strategic value systems across the organization becomes the first and foremost objective of the organization learning process. There exist several other common barriers to organizational learning by the global organizations. For example, the responsibility for promoting organizational learning may not have been well-defined; rewards within the organization may bear no linkage with adopting global strategies; and there may exist no or limited incentives to transfer of learning. In order to make organizational learning a key pursuit in the organization, the responsibility of global HR function is to ensure that such reward and incentive systems are put in place. It has to address the issues of career structure and cross-cultural competence in the organization. It has to be made sure that the HR function is fully involved in giving direction to the processes of employee selection and location so that due attention is given to the diffusion of organizational learning processes.

The Focus of Global HR Functions

It is clear from the above that HR function in a global organization is multifaceted. While aligned to the local HR needs at different geographical entities, the HR functions also have an important global dimension. This has to address the issues of performance appraisals, communication strategies, approach to management development and organization structures.

The performance appraisal processes in global organizations should be focused not only on convergence of current performance with long-term corporate objectives, but also on ensuring that due attention is given to rewarding those who nurture global mindset and organizational learning.

Mention was made earlier of the communication links in a global organization. The global HR function has to make sure that the advantage of local communication styles is utilized to the fullest extent possible by encouraging the same at local levels. At the same time, it has to strive for a common link, an integrating framework which embraces all these local communication links. Equally important is the need to establish climate for global information sharing across diverse geographical entities. This would also include encouraging informal communication channels.

The global HR function must encourage global mobility and provide ways and means of doing so. Global mobility is a credible route to developing global mindset in the organization. Approaches such as cross-border job swaps, transfers and assigning individual managers to global task forces and project teams promote global mobility. Care should be taken however that these global mobility opportunities are not confined to managers belonging to a few nationalities; instead, all persons with potential have the opportunity to form part of such assignments. In the long run, this will be a more effective diffuser of organization-wide common values. The global HR function should also be fully involved in decisions regarding assigning the expatriate staff to manage geographical entities. Not only it should ensure that such opportunities are spread out to more and more talented people, it should also strive that the persons assigned such responsible positions have the requisite stature and quality to be acceptable in the milieu of the geographical entity to which they are assigned.

Lest one is given to an illusion that global organizations have to be necessarily large and complex structures with multiple layers of hierarchy, it has to be pointed out that the need for innovative organizations forms is even greater for global organizations. While the local units have structures which suit their functional requirements, they should also be organized in network modes as much as possible to ensure flexibility. Task forces and flexible teams focused on results are important ingredients of these local organization structures. The philosophy at global level is even more oriented towards having simple flat structures with limited residual hierarchy which can't be done away with. Emphasis at the global level should be given to creating flexible networks of relationships amongst the individual entities, which address the need for developing sense of common identity and value systems amongst them.

Knowledge Management: An Imperative for Global Organizations

Reference was made earlier in this chapter on explicit and tacit knowledge and the need for global organizations to have mechanisms for sharing both these types of knowledge. These concerns legitimately form part of the relatively new discipline of Knowledge Management, and there is no doubt that the concepts of knowledge management are more relevant to a global organization than a purely local one. By its very nature, a global organization has its human resources spread across various geographical boundaries. These human resources themselves are the reservoirs of vast amount of knowledge which is created as a result of the various organization related functions performed by them. Be it R&D, marketing, operations, finance or even strategic planning, performance of tasks for each function requires resorting to a knowledge base, and at the same time, generating new knowledge. It is true that a very large part of the knowledge resides in the brains of people; is intangible; is manifested in the forms of beliefs, attitudes and perceptions; yet the challenge lies in explicating a part of this knowledge and then making that explicit knowledge available for other parts of the organization for better performing their functions. This challenge is manifold in global organizations because of the sheer diversity of its operations and the diversity of human resources and the sources of their tacit knowledge. Not only is the explication of such diverse tacit knowledge difficult, it is equally challenging to make other parts of the organization accept the contention that the knowledge derived from other sources would be useful to their operations. Moreover, the ability to relate this newly explicated tacit knowledge from other sources to their own context, learning from it and adapting it to their local needs is even more uncommon.

The infrastructure part of knowledge management is fairly easier, though not without the attendant concerns that it may remain underutilized. Most global organizations have today established information technology based knowledge management systems which capture, store, share and disseminate explicit knowledge from one place to another in the organization. Much of this explicit knowledge is in the form of computerized databases, and may flow out of assorted information technology applications such as Data-warehousing, Enterprise Resource Planning and Customer Relationship Management, etc. Often, custom-designed knowledge repositories and portals are put in place which is concerned with those organization-specific knowledge artifacts which are not the outputs of traditional IT applications mentioned above. Equally important components of these knowledge management infrastructures are the networks through which the knowledge is transmitted. Use of organization-specific intranets in such communication networks is fairly common, and the combined systems of knowledge portals, repositories and networks become the media for global organizations to create documentations of best practices and share them across geographical entities.

Global organizations these days are well supported by groupware or what is more appropriately called "computer-supported collaborative work". These information technology based systems provide the various geographical entities of a global organization to exchange knowledge on a real time basis. Interactions, which might be faceless (if only messaging options are made use of), or where faces of the collaborators can be identified (where, for instance, video-messaging/conferencing is also used), provide the diversely located human resources to create new and innovative products faster, thereby minimizing the turnaround time and being more responsive to both global and local market needs. These collaborative tools, coupled with the infrastructure of knowledge repositories and networks, also facilitate quick problem solving through sharing of solutions to similar problems faced in the past by some part of the global organization, which some other part might be facing today. They might not be aware of such past problems and solutions already found. Thus, such knowledge management infrastructures provide the requisite resilience to global organizations in avoiding dissipation of valuable resources in solving already solved problems, and instead, directing their energies to demands for more innovative tasks.

The concept of communities of practice as understood in the discipline of knowledge management has taken a new meaning in the context of global organizations. As by their very nature, global organizations are widely dispersed geographically, it is inconceivable that face-to-face interactive sessions will take place amongst them very frequently (though infrequent global information sharing events are actually recommended for global organizations, as mentioned earlier). The communities of practice in their case therefore usually tend to share knowledge through virtual interest groups, which may follow varying rules and conventions regarding contents, periodicity and protocols for knowledge sharing. Some of these interest groups may actually encompass people from outside the formal boundaries of the organization, and cover, for instance, vendors, customers and intermediaries in the supply chain sharing common interests in pursuit of knowledge in the subjects of their choice. Many a times, these networks tend to be quite informal, spontaneous, voluntary in membership, and providing freedom to vary the intensity of interactions they propose to have; though, they are still governed by several well-defined rules/do's and don'ts in order that the networking facilities are not misused. In such cases, they may also become marketing networks and collaborative mechanisms for people who want something X and possess something Y with people who want something Y and possess something X.

Organizational Learning, Learning Organizations and Knowledge Management

The distinction between knowledge management, learning organizations and organizational learning has tended to become increasingly blurred with time. In any case, these distinctions existed because the initiators of these concepts had different time horizons as well as focus. The concepts of organizational learning have been in existence at least from the times of Chris Argyris and Donald Schon, when they dwelt upon the phenomena of single-loop and double-loop learning in organizations. The basic hypothesis floated by these authors was that every person is guided by mental maps/theories which guide his/her actions, and that these theories are actually different from those explicitly espoused by him. Effectiveness results from developing congruence between these two sets of theory (theory-in-use and espoused theory); and the gap between them creates a dynamic for reflection and dialogue. Where the consequences of actions by individuals are different from what was desired, it is clear that there exists a mismatch between intention and outcome. There may be two responses to this mismatch, each type of response corresponding to the notion of either single-loop or double-loop learning. Under the domain of single-loop learning, the remedial action is to develop a strategy which however is confined to the existing strategic understanding of the external and internal environment. However, too often, a single-loop learning model doesn't work, since it has failed to address the fundamental issues of changing the strategic environment itself. It is here that the notion of double-loop learning comes into play. In this scenario, even the strategic environment is questioned, and the identified solution may well be the modification of an organization's underlying norms, policies and objectives. Ironically, many organizations remain confined to the solutions offered by single-loop learning, even when it is increasingly clear that in such organizational situations, double-loop learning might be most needed. These authors (of the present book) are not aware of any organizational research which might establish whether the global organizations talked about in this chapter are relatively focused more on single-loop or double-loop learning. However, it is apparent that the chances of single-loop learning not delivering the results and the need to increasingly focus on double-loop learning might be greater for global organizations.

Henk W. Volberda in his classical book, "Building the Flexible Firm—How to Remain Competitive" (first published in 1998) extends this discussion of single-loop and double-loop learning further. According to him, single-loop learning goes together with the development of routines and standard operating procedures, which are institutionalized in the planning and control systems and shared values of the organization. On the other hand, double-loop learning is necessitated by the need to unlearn past routines in order to become more receptive to new possibilities. This becomes important when totally new values and norms are required for the organization, and past experience may not provide any advantage; and the organization is required to have the ability to adjust its overall rules and norms. The incompatible organizational norms are resolved by setting new priorities and weighing norms or by restructuring the norms themselves. However, he also cautions against excessive double-loop learning, as it may lead to a situation of lack of a clear strategy. This may actually create instability in the organization, and eventually, the organization may end up as a chaotic one that can't retain a sense of identity and continuity over time. He then introduces the concept of deutro-learning, which essentially is the art of balancing single-loop learning and double-loop learning in the organization. A deutro-learning organization reflects on and inquires into previous contexts for learning, and tries to maintain an appropriate balance between the single-loop and double-loop learning.

Valuable as these concepts of organizational learning are, they have been overshadowed by the well-known principles of a learning organization, propounded by Peter Senge through his classical, "Fifth Discipline". Since these are already dealt with elaborately in the current management literature, no attempt is made here to reflect further on them. Suffice it to say that a learning organization is something like a role model, which is in a perpetual learning and sharing mode; wherein the cultural and internal environmental factors are conducive to such sharing of knowledge; and where personal mastery is sought to be enhanced to the cutting edge level through knowledge sharing.

Knowledge Management as a discipline, on the other hand, is primarily an outcome of the push given by information technology developments, which enabled development of workable systems for documenting organizational knowledge and sharing it within the organization as well as with other external stakeholders. The pursuit has been towards what might be called "zero latency", meaning that information/knowledge once generated in any part of an organization is almost instantaneously available in its all other parts, howsoever separately they might be located geographically or otherwise. The proponents of knowledge management, however, recognized fairly early in the game that this sharable explicit knowledge is the proverbial tip of the iceberg, and the real challenge lies in understanding the vast quantum of tacit knowledge. Even today, the literature of KM is concerned with this issue of understanding and tackling tacit knowledge. Not only that, the cultural barriers to knowledge sharing and the need for developing appropriate reward systems for sharing knowledge are confronting designers and implementers of knowledge management systems. Imagine the magnitude of these barriers in the context of a large global organization, where multiple regions, nationalities and communities are at work, and where colossal diversity itself makes these barriers not easily surmountable.

Flexibility and Global Organizations

A reference may also be made to the concepts of organizational flexibility even though the concept of 'flexibility' may appear obvious, it is worthy of serious research investigation, both in terms of possibilities and contents. Several persons are working on this. It would be important to distinguish between various forms of flexibility and their interdependence. For example, one could confine oneself to operational flexibility—the ability to perform tasks with alternative options, which may be appropriate as per the demands of the situation. One could extend this further to what may be termed as structural flexibility, wherein alternative options can be explored to change structural variables in order to achieve results. The third, more widely encompassed level of flexibility is what might be called strategic flexibility, which also explores further options of changing the strategic dimensions of doing business. The issue of debate is not whether a limited level of flexibility is good enough for an organization, but it is the ability to decide what is most appropriate for the organization as a whole. In that context, this idea is somehow linked with single-loop, double-loop and deutro-learning mentioned earlier.

For a global organization, which faces enormous challenges because it is simultaneously exposed to diverse cultures, technologies and human resources, the importance of all the three forms of flexibility mentioned above can't be overemphasized. In fact, a global organization has to resort to multiple responses simultaneously in different parts of its structure. At some places, mere readjustment of operational details in accordance with well-established best practices may be sufficient. At some other places, organizational design and other structural changes may be necessary to enable greater sharing, while at some other places, it may be necessary to have a re-look at the strategic dimensions, and make it more in conformity with the global strategic direction set by the top management.

Fortunately, enough empirical evidence exists to establish that information technology is a strong enabler of organizational flexibility in all its forms, whether, operational or structural or strategic. This has already been discussed in an earlier chapter in the context of impact of information technology on organizational structure and processes. This enabling characteristic of information technology is actually a boon for global organizations because they have a better discretion to exercise changes in their internal operations and deliverables to the customers, and take due advantage of their global nature. That was in any case the reason for setting up global organization in the first place.

Chapter 13

Longitudinal Thinking: An Action Perspective

There is a differentiation between growth and development. Growth, as is recognized, consists of an increase in substance, usually manifested by a proliferation of the structures already present. It is essentially continuous and quantitative in character, but can proceed in the absence of new structures only up to a point. Development, as is agreed, consists of an increase in structure, which is manifested by emergence of new structural forms and very often has a qualitative character. This is of course in an organizational context. In the larger macro economic form, growth has been extended to cover areas of economic dimensions and is measured in terms of GDP. Development is a much wider concept and covers concepts of human welfare and 'happiness quantum' in certain cases. To get into that debate is not the purpose of this analysis but to provide the backdrop in which longitudinal thinking can be understood.

The present state, as defined by Vinayshil Gautam, is a result of the past state and the future state would be the result of the present state and the choices made today. This phenomenon is known as longitudinal thinking. Put simply longitudinal thinking helps to see the roots and antecedents of the present state of affairs and thereby strengthen the search for better solutions and better forms. Many have seen longitudinal thinking in terms of applied research and have talked of it as phenomena which cover repeated observations of the same items over long periods. There are some other definitions of longitudinal thinking and as D. Mirrors and P.H. Frisen in his paper on *Longitudinal Analysis of Organizations*:

A Methodological Perspective has talked of, it is "those techniques and methodologies and activities which permit the observation, description and/or classification of organizational phenomena in such a way that process can be identified and empirically documented". Vinayshil Gautam believes that longitudinal thinking helps one to see the roots and impacting factors thereby helping to atomize the legacy variables. The advantage of this is that the legacy can be selectively decomposed into those elements which retard growth and those which accelerate growth. The elements which retard growth are to be eliminated and the elements which accelerate growth are to be strengthened. This means that any intervention for better preparation for the future can then integrate on to and be imbedded in what already exists. Operationally, longitudinal studies have been applied in many fields. In Sociology, study of life events through life time help to generate a pattern. Longitudinal studies are particularly useful in understanding the nature of evolution and the critical points of change.

There are people who have argued that there are different classes of longitudinal studies such as Cohort Study, Trend Study, Panel Study etc. Cohort Study requires subjects of a particular treatment being followed over a period of time and compared with another group who are not affected by the conditions under investigation. In Organizational Study, for example, people of same time length, education doing similar jobs could be a Cohort. This analysis requires measuring of some characteristics of one or more Cohorts at multiple points of time. In this manner, effects can be better mapped. This is about life history as mentioned earlier. In a Trend Study, information is generated about the aggregate net changes without manipulating the variable. Pre-Electoral opinion polls are interesting illustration.

However, to find out the gross changes not to overlook the net changes, what is required is a Panel Study. This measures the same sample of respondents at various points of time. This is very useful for mapping shifting attitudes and changing patterns of behaviour.

Given the fact that change can be discontinuous in nature in organizations marked by a series of jumps from one level of organisation to the next, one has to be careful. Discontinuity here is referring to the sharpness of transition which results out of increase in scale.

Many would agree that amongst the pervasive problems confronted by present-day organisations, number, increasing complexity, accelerated change, rapid technological advances, reliance on standardised strategies. Some organisations deal with this successfully, others crumble. Increasing complexity is difficult to scientifically analyse; accelerated change leaves people dazed; rapid technological advances call for high learning ability; standardisation does havoc to contextual factors.

Clearly such an organisation is a malfunctioning organisation. The symptoms quickly come to the fore. Employee spirits are blunted. Management struggles to keep going. Decision makers have problems of group identity and ego. Increasing number and uncertainty of crisis events leave several in the organisation with a sense of insecurity. There can be both genuine and studied helplessness. In an environment of declining performance and growing deterioration imaginative accounting is resorted to.

There is a need to recognise the positive organisations, systems and associations. There is a need to encourage the adaptive organisation that is open to ideas and perceptions also from the outside. One has to be alert to the present and likely future trends, learn from other's experiences and not convert oneself to an experimental menu. One has to be quick to respond, but restrained in reaction. Some of the major approaches to the management of organisations remain: Classical, Scientific, Behavioural, Socio-Technical, Operations Research Oriented, Information Systems Oriented, Systems Oriented and more. It may be unnecessary to swear by anyone of them and sanguine to realise that all these approaches put together are what a situation requires. Ultimately, the indicator of the modern times is variety and rapidity, and this needs flexibility coupled with a set of core values of integrity and non-malleability.

Resilience which is the ability to absorb and bounce back from external shocks is a permutation that has to go hand in hand with *homeo statis*, which is the maintenance of constancy of the internal environment. The truth of life experience is symbiosis. For those who recognise this beautiful word would be aware that symbiosis is said to exist between two subsystems when neither can exist without the other. However, living systems have the capability of the decreasing entropy. One should, forever be a part of the growth and development process.

There is a need, as noted earlier, to recognise the distinction between processes of growth and development and have the ability to distinguish between the two. There are various sources of growth and they are very often cut short by a crisis or ellie of some variety. Illustratively, creativity is a source of growth. It is often terminated by a crisis of leadership. Ability to give direction is a source of growth. It is terminated by a crisis of autonomy. The answer lies, as already noted in the creation and strengthening of an adaptive organisation. This requires looking for organisations that encourage loosening up. It requires a search of organisations which is tolerant of variety and avoids strict controls. The challenge for such organisations would be in matching all this with a bottom line of standards and ensconing it in an environment of quality. Anticipation of potential crisis in these organisations is matched by their pre-planned management. In this lies the essence of their capacity to cope with change.

Growth demands change and that is most effective when aided by longitudinal thinking. Environmental processes demand change, optimisation of technological variables demand change, emerging economic variables demand change, maintenance of position of excellence demands change, objectives demand change. In short, life itself demands change. Change comes because the structure of knowledge changes as do its content. Attitudes need sharpening and behaviour needs modifications, just in the same way as cognitive systems require transformation. They all stand owned and disowned in various measures. Ultimately, it is your funeral or salvation. You must learn to choose, choose consciously, choose wisely and be responsible for your choices. You must have learnt the technique of lateral thinking to enable all this.

There is a need to recognise that there is a life beyond lateral thinking. There is a need to go beyond lateral thinking and also do longitudinal thinking.

Each one of us is a product of some heritage variables — our genes, our environmental conditioning, early childhood experiences. I have known of adults, who over thirty years of their adult life could not get themselves to learn how to close a lid, close a bottle or for that matter put a cap on any object. Such is the terrifying experience of the "inherited variable", which goes into making of all of us. Organisations are no different.

The answer lies as pointed out and earlier in breaking down our variable of the tradition and fusing it with modern. The banal has to be rejected and positive retained.

The most important thing is to recognise the issue of the fusion of the modern and the traditional. To manage change is to register that neither modernity nor tradition, are any longer local phenomenon. In the era of globalisation, whether labour or capital travels or not, concepts certainly travel and have a universal dimension. This is natural because information revolution has strengthened and accelerated communication of ideas and concepts.

In view of the fact that, management is the art of the practitioner, globally people have been looking for ideas, which work, and strategies which produce results. The discipline itself is a quest for effectiveness.

Gradually, it is being recognised that effectiveness as managers is rooted in effectiveness as persons just as much as effectiveness of the systems is rooted in the vibrant nature of the context. To contend with change, which is the law of life, is the basic issue, and this every human being faces. This every organisation faces. This requires special craft.

The human being faces fewer levels of change than what the manager does. 'Management Wisdom' is arrived at partly from empiricism and partly reinterpretation and application of the certain conventional disciplines in their scholastic traditions. As a system, Assyrian historical records, the Egyptian management practices, the Arab sophistication in decision making processes have a compendium of management strategies that have been periodically researched on and often eluded to, but rarely have they been built into a real world dynamic HRD architecture.

The charisma of the electronic revolution, the dazzle of the armorial superiority of post-industrial West and the sheer decisiveness of hard currency operations have made the protagonist of traditional wisdom not only defensive but at times apologetic. This has left both the modernists and the traditionalist somewhat isolated in watertight compartment in the world of management. Neither has been able to wield sufficient power in the absence of a synergistic integration. In the meantime, modernity itself has developed its own tradition and the modernity of tradition has similarly tendered to be overlooked.

There are number of situations which can be tricky in the quest of organizational effectiveness. For one, people often mouth opinion which they perhaps neither believe nor understand, if not both. Hence using the same phenomena over a period of time for longitudinal analysis can be a problem. Similarly with the best of functions, the population which prospects in longitudinal analysis could change over a period of time. As B.C. Sutradhar in his text "Analysing Ordinal Longitudinal Survey Data : Generalize Estimating Equations Approach" says 'one of the main goals of longitudinal survey is then to describe the marginal expectation of ordinal polytomous outcome variable as a function of covariates while accounting for the structural as well as longitudinal correlations. The structural correlations come from the polytomous nature of the response variable, and the longitudinal correlations from the repetition of the polytomous responses over time.' Clearly the application of longitudinal thinking, as noted earlier, has been in large range of discipline and organizational study can be considerably enriched by drawing upon the lessons of its use elsewhere.

One thing that is clear is that in studying organizational issues, exclusive use of either quantitative tools or qualitative perspective will yield inconclusive results. The two have to be carried out together in tandem. The perspective of longitudinal thinking if carried out holistically will heighten many times, the range and depth of organizational analysis and thereby organizational effectiveness.

Bibliography

Abelon, Daniel & Hilpert, Edwin J., "Communication in the Modem Corporate Environment", Prentice Hall, 1996.

Allen I. Krant (Ed.), "Organisational Surveys: Tools for Assessment and Change", Jossey-Bass Publications, 1996.

Andrew H. V. and Huber G.P. (1990). "Longitudinal Field Research Methods for Studying Processes of Organizational Change," *Organization Change*, Vol. 1, No. 3, pp. 213-219.

Anthony, P.D., "The Ideology of Work", Tavistock Publications, 1977.

Argyris, Chris, "Integrating the Individual and the Organisation", John Wiley & Sons Inc., New York, 1964.

Arundale, R. (1980). "Studying Change Over Time: Criteria for Sampling From Continuous Variables", *Communication Research*, Vol. 7, pp. 227-263.

Ashkenas, Ron; Ulrich, Dave; Jick, Todd & Kerr Steve, "The Boundaryless Organisation: Breaking the Chains of Organisational Structure", Jossey-Bass Publishers, 1998.

Bartlett, Christopher A. & Ghosal, Sumantara, "Transnational Management - Text, Cases & Readings in Cross-Border Management", IRWIN, 1995.

Beer, Stafford, "The Heart of Enterprise", Penguin Press, London, 1975.

Bennis, Warren, "21st Century Organisation: Reinventing through Reengineering", Jossey-Bass Publishers, 1997.

Betts, Stephen C. (2003), "Contingency Theory: Science Or Technology?", *Journal of Business and Economic Research*, Vol. 1, No. 8, pp. 123-130.

Cameron, Kim S. and Whetten, David, A., "Organisational

Effectiveness: A Comparison of Multiple Models", Academic Press, New York, 1983.

Chen, G.; Jamieson, J.M.; Schkade, L.L. and Smith, C. H. - "The General Theory of Systems Applied to Management and Organisation", Intersystems Publications, New York, 1980.

Chevalier, Franciose and Segalla, Michael (Ed) – "Organisational Behaviour and Change in Europe: Case Studies", Sage Publications, 1996.

Cohen, Allan R.; Fink, Stephen C.; Gadon, Herman and Willits, Robin D. – "Effective Behaviour in Organisations", Richard D. Irwin Inc., Illinois, 1976.

Clutterbuck, David, "The Power of Empowerment", Kogen Page, 1994.

Coulson-Thomas Colin, "The Future of the Organisation: Achieving Excellence through Business Transformation", Kogen Page, 1997.

D'Aprix, Roger, "Communicating for Change: Connecting the Work Place with Market Place", Jossey-Bass Publications, 1996.

Davidson, Mike, "The Transformation of Management", McMillan Business, 1995.

De Greene, Kenyon, B., "The Adaptive Organisation: Anticipation and Management of Crisis", John Wiley & Sons, New York, 1981.

Demystifying & Applying Knowledge Management in UNDP — ESCAP-UNDP KM workshop, 7 March 2005, Bangkok.

Dickson, Tim (Ed.), "Mastering Global Business", Prentice Hall, London, 1999.

Edward, P. A., Goudy J.W. and Keith M.P. (1978). "Congruence between Panel and Recall Data in "Longitudinal Research", *Public Opinion Quarterly*, June, pp. 380-389.

Ferreira, S.D.M. and M. Neto, (2005), "Knowledge management and social learning exploring the cognitive dimension of development", Volume 1(3), 4-17.

Ferrell, Mary Zey (Ed.), "Readings on Dimensions of Organisations: Environment, Context, Structure, Process and -Performance", Good Year Publishing Company, California, 1979.

Flood, R.L. and Jackson, M.C., "Cybernetics and Organisation Theory - A Critical Review", Cybernetics and Systems, No. 1, Vol. 14, 1988. Hemisphere Publishing Corporation, New York, 1988.

Fortuin, F. and Omta, S.W.F. (2006). "Aligning R&D to Business Strategy - A Longitudinal Study from 1997 to 2002", *Proceedings of the 39th Hawaii International Conference on System Sciences*, pp. 1-8.

Gautam, Vinayshil, "Comparative Manpower Planning Practices: Select Indian Experiences", National Publishing House, New Delhi, 1988.

Gautam, Vinayshil, "Issues in Organisation Management: Predilections & Potential", Global Business Press, New Delhi, 1992, 25.

Gautam, Vinayshil (1999). "Towards Longitudinal Thinking", *Abhigyan*, Vol. XVII, No. 3, Editorial.

Gautam, Vinayshil (2000). "Longitudinal Thinking", *Abhigyan*, Vol. XVIII, No. 1, Editorial.

Gautam, Vinayshil and Sinha, S. (2004). *Understanding Telecom Management*. New Delhi: Concept Publishing Company (P) Ltd.

Gautam, Vinayshil, "Impact of Computerisation on Work Design", *Productivity*, Vol. XXVIII, Jan-Mar 1988, New Delhi.

Giardini, A. and Kabst, R. (2008). Effects of Work-Family Human Resource Practices: A Longitudinal Perspective", *The International Journal of Human Resource Management*, Vol. 19, No. 11, pp. 2079–2094.

Gupta, Jatinder N.D.; and Sharma, Sushil, K., "Creating Knowledge-based Organizations", Idea Group Publishing, 2004.

Gupta, P.P., "Managing Innovations: The CMC Experience", *Indian Journal of Training and Development*, pp. 10-12, Vol. XVII, No. 4, July-August 1987.

Gurbaxani, Vijay and Whang, Seungjin, "The Impact of Information Systems on Organisations and Markets", Communications of the ACM, January 1991, Vo. 34, No. 1 (pp. 59-73).

Haines III Y.V. (2010). "A Longitudinal Analysis (1975-2005) of the Evolution of the Human Resources Profession", *Industrial Relations*, Vol. 65, No. 3, pp. 491-513.

Hall, Richard H. (Ed.), "Formal Organisation", Basic Beks Inc. Publishers, New York 1972.

Harris, Thomas A., "I am OK, you are OK", Harper and Row, New York, 1967.

Harrison, G.A., "Human Adaptation", Oxford Science Publication, 1993.

Hellriegel, D. and Slocum, W., "Organisational Behaviour - Contingency Views", St. Paul, West Publishing, 1976.

Hersey, Paul and Blanchard, Kenneth H., "Management of Organisational Behaviour", Prentice Hall of India, 1977.

Hodge, B.J. and Anthony, Williams P., "Organisation Theory", Allyn and Bacon Inc. Boston, 1984.

Hrebiniak, Lawrence, G., "Complex Organisations", West Publishing Co., 1978.

Huber, George P., "A Theory of the Effects of Advances Information, Technologies on Organisational Design, Intelligence and Decision Making", The Academy of Management Review, Vol. 13, No. 3, July 1988.

Jacinta M. Gau (2010). "A Longitudinal Analysis of Citizens' Attitudes about Police", *International Journal of Police Strategies & Management*, Vol. 33, No. 2, pp. 236-252.

Jackson, John H; Morgan, Cyril P. and Paolillo, Joseph G. - "Organisation Theory: A Macro - perspective for Management", Prentice Hall, Englewood Cliffs, New Jersey, 1986.

Jarillo, J.C., "Strategic Networks: Creating the Borderless Organisation", Butterworth Heinnemann, 1993.

Johnson, Mike, "Managing in the Next Millenium", Butterworth Heinemann, 1995.

Jones, Gareth R. (2001), "*Organizational Theory, Text and Cases*", Third Edition, Pearson Education.

Khandwalla, Pradip N., "The Design of Organisations", N.Y. Harcourt Brace, Jovanovich, 1977.

Koontz, Harold; O'Donnel Cyril and Weihrich, Heinz, "Management", McGraw Hill International Book Co., Auckland, 1984.

Kotter, John P., "Organisation Dynamics: Diagnosis and Intervention", Addison Wesley Publishing Co., New York, 1978.

Lacey, R., Kennett-Hensel, P.A. (2010). "Longitudinal Effects of Corporate Social Responsibility on Customer Relationships", *Journal of Business Ethics*, Vol. 97, pp. 581–597.

Lahiri, Sugato, "Learning via Lab", Business World, 6-19 Nov. 1991.

Leavitt, H.J; Dill, William, R. and Eyring, Henry B., "The Organisation World: A Systems View of Management".

Litterer, Joseph A. (Ed.), "Organisations: Systems, Controls and Adaptation", Vol. I & Vol. II, John Wiley & Sons Inc., New York, 1963.

Litterer, Joseph A., "The Analysis of Organisations", John Wiley & Sons, New York, 1965.

Livingston, W.L., "The New Plague: Organisations in Complexity, FES Limited Publisher, New York, 1984.

"Longitudinal Study", published in Wikkipedia, Available at: http://en.wikipedia.org/wiki/Longitudinal_study, Retrieved on December 3, 2010.

Maira, Arun &, Scott-Morgan Peter B., "The Accelerating Organisation: Embracing the Human Face of Change", McGraw Hill, 1996.

March, J.G. and Simon, H.A., "Organisations", John Wiley & Sons, New York, 1958.

Martin Hahn (2007), Contingency Theory at http://en.articles gratuits. com/contingency-theory-id1620.php

Michalski, Walter J. & King, Dana J. (Ed.), "40 Tools for Cross-functional Teams: Building Synergy for Breakthrough Creativity", Productivity Press, 1998.

Miller, James G., "Living Systems Theory", McGraw Hill Book Co., New York, 1978.

Miller, D. and Friesen, P.H. (1982). "The Longitudinal Analysis of Organizations: A Methodological Perspective," *Management Science*, Vol. 28, No. 9, pp. 1013-1034.

Miller, Katherine, "Organisational Communications: Approaches and Procedures", Wordsworth Publishing Co., 1995.

More, E.A. and Laird, R.K., "Organisations in the Communications Age: An Introduction to Organisational Communication and Communication Technology for Management", Pergamon Press, Sydney, 1985.

Morgan, Gareth, "Images of Organisations", Sage Publications, 1986.

Murdick, Robert G., Ross Joel E. and Claggett, James R., "Information Systems for Modern Management", Prentice Hall of India, New Delhi, 1988.

Narayan, S., "Select Dimensions of Organisational Effectiveness in Coal India Limited - A Diagnostic Study", Ph. D. Thesis submitted to Centre for Management Studies, IIT, New Delhi, 1985.

Nash, Michael, "Managing Organisational Performance", Jossey Bash Publishers, 1983.

Newstorm, John & Scannell, Edward, "The Big Book of Team Building Games: Trust-Building Activities, Team Spirit, Exercises and other Fun Things to do", McGraw Hill, 1998.

Notings from the November 1987 International Training and Development Conference, Delhi, *Indian Journal of Training and Development*, pp. 43-48, Vol. XVII, No. 6, Nov-Dec. 1987.

Phelps, C.C. (2010). "Longitudinal Study of the Influence of Alliance Network Structure and Composition on Firm Exploratory Innovation", *Academy of Management Journal*, Vol. 53, No. 4, pp. 890–913.

Phillips, Jack J., "Accountability in Human Resource Management", Gulf Publishing Co., 1996.

Porras, J., and Berg, P. (1978). "Evaluation Methodology in Organization Development: An Analysis and Critique", *Journal of Applied Behavioral Science*, Vol. 14, pp. 151-173.

Pucik Vladimir, Tichy Noel M. and Barnett, Carole K. (Ed.), "Globalising Management: Creating and Leading the Competitive Organisation", John Wiley & Sons Inc., 1993.

Savage, Charles M., "Fifth Generation Management", Prentice Hall of India Pvt. Ltd., New Delhi, 1992.

Schein, Edgar, "Organisational Psychology", Prentice Hall of India, New Delhi, 1969.

Sharma, R.A., "Organisation Theory and Behaviour", Tata McGraw Hill, 1982.

Shockley-Zalabak, Pamela, "Foundations of Organisational Communications: Knowledge, Sensitivity, Skills, Values", Longman, 1991.

Smith, M. K. (2001), "Chris Argyris: theories of action, double-loop learning and organizational learning", the Encyclopedia of Informal Education, www.infed.org/ thinkers/argyris.htm.

Sutradhar, B.C. (2000). "Analyzing Ordinal Longitudinal Survey Data: Generalized estimating equations approach," *Biometrika*, Vol. 87, No. 4, pp. 837–848.

Takeuchi, N. and Takeuchi, T. (2009). "A Longitudinal Investigation on the Factors Affecting Newcomers' Adjustment: Evidence from Japanese Organizations", *The International Journal of Human Resource Management*, Vol. 20, No. 4, pp. 928-952.

Tamotia, S.K. and Gautam, Vinayshil (2005). "Essays in Longitudinal Thinking: Managing Change with Continuity". New Delhi: Concept Publishing Company.

Tannenbaum, Arnold S., "Control in Organisations", McGraw Hill Book Co., New York, 1968.

Tiwana, Amrit, "The Knowledge Management Toolkit: Orchestrating IT, Strategy and Knowledge Platforms", Pearson Education, 2002.

Tripathi, P.C., "Successful Organisation Management - Effective Strategies for Managing Organisations Successfully", Global Business Press, New Delhi, 1992.

Twisk, J. and Vente, W. (2002). "Attrition in Longitudinal Studies: How to Deal with Missing Data", *Journal of Clinical Epidemiology*, Vol. 55, pp. 329-337.

Volberda, Henk W., "Building the Flexible Firm: How to remain competitive", Oxford University Press, Oxford, 1998.

Westrum, Ron and Samaha, Khalil, "Complex Organisations: Growth, Struggle and Change", Prentice Hall Inc. Englewood Cliffs, New Jersey, 1984.

White, Donald D. and Vroman, H. William, "Action in Organisations: Cases and Experiences in Organisational Behaviour", Holbrook Press Inc., Boston, 1977.

Whyte, William H., "The Organisation Man", Penguin Books, 1956.

Wieland, George F. and Ullrich, Robert A., "Organisations: Behaviour, Design and Change", Richards Irwin Inc., Illinois, 1970.

Index